MW00325587

"If Jonathan Edwards's *The End for W[...]* defined Reformed teleology and escha[...] Lodahl's *Renewal in Love* has the pote[...] [...] [...] same for the Wesleyan tradition but also register Wesley's vision in the broader theological landscape and reorient the conversation altogether. God's glory is not compromised but illumined even brighter in the light of a creation perfected in divine love."

—Amos Yong
Professor of Theology and Mission
Fuller Theological Seminary

"This is Wesleyan theology at its best—nurtured in dialogue; full of wisdom from Scripture, the long Christian tradition, and study of God's creation; and presented in a winsome, loving spirit."

—Randy L. Maddox
William Kellon Quick Professor of Wesleyan and Methodist Studies
Duke Divinity School

"Following a close analysis of biblical texts and the writings of John Wesley, the authors offer a theological anthropology that explores what it means to be made in God's image and to image God. Both earthly oriented and divinely focused, this book challenges readers to live lives of love in the light of God's purpose for this world. I plan to tote it along with me to reread on my next nature hike!"

—Thomas Jay Oord
Professor of Theology and Philosophy
Northwest Nazarene University

"This is a delightfully insightful interconnection of themes from throughout the Old and New Testaments, historical theology, and today. The authors ease readers into the thought world of the Scriptures and the way early theologians echoed those thoughts. They then bring it all forward into practical implications within the complexities of our present life in the world. These authors have given us all a gift to clearly know who we humans are gifted to be in the world in the face of God and God's redeeming work in Christ."

—Eric Vail
Assistant Professor of Theology
Mount Vernon Nazarene University
Author of *Creation and Chaos Talk: Charting a Way Forward*

"This profound work treats troubling questions about the Bible and the world theologically and socially without pretending to provide once-and-for-all answers. And yet it does provide cogent, carefully contemplated principles emphasizing the critical role of our cooperation with God—how God needs us to continue renewing the world in love. In this we follow our incarnate Lord and Savior, Jesus Christ, who, in bringing healing salvation to all creation, shows us how to live in God's image."

—Karen Strand Winslow
Professor of Biblical Studies
Azusa Pacific Seminary

RENEWAL IN LOVE

RENEWAL IN LOVE

Living Holy Lives in God's Good Creation

MICHAEL LODAHL &
APRIL CORDERO MASKIEWICZ

BEACON HILL PRESS
OF KANSAS CITY

Copyright © 2014 by Michael Lodahl and April Cordero Maskiewicz
Beacon Hill Press of Kansas City
PO Box 419527
Kansas City, MO 64141
www.BeaconHillBooks.com

ISBN 978-0-8341-3358-7

Printed in the
United States of America

Cover Design: Grace Oldon
Interior Design: Sharon Page

Library of Congress Cataloguing-in-Publication Data

Lodahl, Michael E., 1955-
    Renewal in love : living holy lives in God's good creation / Michael Lodahl and April Cordero Maskiewicz.
      pages cm
    Includes bibliographical references.
    ISBN 978-0-8341-3358-7 (pbk.)
    1. Theological anthropology—Christianity. 2. Image of God. 3. Regeneration (Theology) 4. Creation. I. Title.
    BT701.3.L63 2014
    233'.5—dc23

                            2014022871

The Internet addresses, email addresses, and phone numbers in this book are accurate at the time of publication. They are provided as a resource. Beacon Hill Press of Kansas City does not endorse them or vouch for their content or permanence.

10 9 8 7 6 5 4 3 2 1

.

For
Dorys Pugong of the Philippines,
Carolyn Leslie White of Great Britain,
Joseph Kisoi of Kenya,
Matthew Seaman of Australia,
Marcos Mujica of the United States, and
Renee Roberts of the People's Republic of Ocean Beach:

six youthful Wesleyan scholars from around the world
whose passion for the redemption of God's creation
makes this aging theologian's heart feel strangely warmed

CONTENTS

Acknowledgments   11

Part I: God, Our Creator   15

1. Renewal in the Image of God   17
   Created in the Image of God   19
   Reading Genesis 1 Theologically   21
   The Image of God as a Divine Calling   29

2. In the Image of the Social God   35
   Divine Wisdom, Divine Word   36
   The Inviting Word of Creation and the Word
      that Became Flesh   41
   Exercising Dominion in the Light of Christ   43
   Augustine's Rule of Interpretation   44
   And on the Seventh Day . . .   49

3. An Everlasting Covenant   50
   Reading Noah's Narrative Theologically   51
   Our Covenantal God   56
   The Fire Next Time?   58
   What Has Happened to the Everlasting Covenant?   60
   The Persistence of Our Covenantal God   64

Part II: God, Our Re-Creator   67

4. Recapitulation and Renewal   69
   The Contribution of Irenaeus:
      Affirming the Goodness of the Body   70
   The Contribution of Gregory of Nazianzus:
      Affirming the Goodness of the Mind   80
   The Contribution of Maximus the Confessor:
      Affirming the Goodness of Volition   86

5. Sanctification as Renewal in Love   93
   The Resurrection of the Incarnate Word   96
   "Renewal in the Image of God" through the Incarnate Word   100
   The Image of God as Love   104
   The Threefold Image of God   108

6. Tending to Creation's Cries   111
   Eschatological Hope and Human Agency   112
   How Will God Redeem Creation?   120
   Liberation for All Creation   123
   What Is God's "End" for the World?   129

Part III: Sabbath   **133**

7. Gathering Up the Fragments *(A Sabbath Meditation)*   135

The Eighth Day   **145**

Notes   **147**

ACKNOWLEDGMENTS

The ideas and arguments that have flowed together into this book first began to emerge in the fall of 2010. It happened while teaching a "God and Nature" course to students from Christian universities doing a semester abroad with the Creation Care Study Program in Nabitunich, Belize. It is eminently appropriate, and deeply satisfying, to have finished the book during a return trip to Central America, this time in Costa Rica. Here I've been privileged to teach a similar course, again to Christian students doing study overseas, for the Quetzal Educational Research Center of Southern Nazarene University. What marvelous bookend experiences!

Many thanks, then, go first to the directors, staff, and students in Belize whose hospitality and love for learning provided that initial inspiration several years ago. Thanks also to my more recent Costa Rica students whose comments and questions helped with the finishing touches on the book: Sydney Bergen, Miranda Garlett, Lesli Kelly, Rachel Rindom, Arwyn Roe, Gentry Smith, and Rebecca Sylvester. *Muchas gracias* for the hospitality of QERC directors Jordan and Megan Young and student intern Addison Martin. (*Y gracias a Dios* for Nancy's cooking!)

Most of the work of writing, of course, occurred in the time between these theological adventures in tropical forests. I am grateful to the Wesleyan Center of my home institution, Point Loma Nazarene University, for several grants during the past few years that supported the research, reflection, and writing involved in this effort. Point Loma also granted me a sabbatical in the fall of 2012 to continue to develop the book's themes.

That 2012 sabbatical turned into a once-in-a-lifetime Asian sojourn for my wife, Janice, and me. In Tokyo and several other beautiful cities of Japan, I preached and lectured on the theme of humanity in the image of God, renewed in Christ. We remember with warm gratitude the Christian hospitality of beloved pastors such as Isaac Saoshiro and Hiroo Kudo; keen translators such as Hiro Furuta, Shoji Nakae, and Nathan the Interpreter; and fellow theologians Makoto Sakamoto and Manabu Ishida, among so many others. Our sincere *arigato* to the Japan Holiness Association for inviting us to come and share in blessings of the gospel of Jesus Christ. It was a joy to lecture on this book's themes also at Kansai Bible College in Kobe, Japan, with the help of my good friend and fellow theologian Shinichi Ozu and the school's deans, Naoto Kamano and Chieko Nishina. Japan now holds a warm, special place in our hearts.

From Japan we journeyed to Asia-Pacific Nazarene Theological Seminary in Manila, Philippines, and fell in love with the school— administration, staff, professors, and students. *Maraming salamat* to the students from all over East Asia whom I was privileged to teach the course "Humanity in the Image of God," continuing to hone this book's argument. Particularly warm gratitude to fellow theologians Dick Eugenio (spouse, Mary Ann, angelic daughter Heloise) and Larnie Sam Tabuena (sweetheart Annabelle), along with seminary deans Floyd Cunningham and San Young Lee for helping to make APNTS our heartfelt home for several months.

During that sabbatical semester we were invited also to visit Korea Nazarene University in Cheonan, South Korea, to share in sermons and lectures some of the ideas explored in chapters 2 and 5 of this book. *Kamsa hamnida* to Churlee Han, dean of the chapel, and university liaison Eunhee Han for their tremendous hospitality. I especially thank fellow theologian Sung-Won Kim for his caring friendship, careful scholarship, and undeniable adventures in Korean cuisine!

Back in the States, I carry a special debt of gratitude for opportunities given to develop the book's ideas for public audiences. Thank you to MidAmerica Nazarene University chaplain Randy Beckum, and librarian Bruce Flanders, for the opportunity to come to the heartland in the spring of 2013 and share ideas from chapter 1. In the fall of 2013 I was privileged to meet with the faculty of Mount Vernon Nazarene University for a day-long seminar and attempt to develop the ideas in chapter 4 toward a holistic Christian pedagogy. Thank you to Mount Vernon psychologist Randy Cronk and fine young theologian Eric Vail, among many others, for their hospitality and encouragement. I especially thank MVNU President Henry Spaulding for his insightful response at the end of the day's proceedings; in the space of a fifteen-minute talk Henry modeled the careful process of taking theological ideas that next crucial step toward actual, living, communal practice.

To my old college and seminary buddy, Chuck Johnstone: thank you, my man, for your rich friendship over the years, sealed in Christian love and ministry. I thank you, also, for allowing me to come and work through many of this volume's ideas with the patient laypeople of San Ramon, California, United Methodist Church. May their longsuffering be rewarded!

Finally, deep gratitude to Point Loma colleague and friend April Cordero Maskiewicz, extraordinary professor of biological and ecological sciences and my co-author. A couple of years ago April heard about the book I had begun and volunteered her help. I quickly and happily accepted. This book is so much better because of April's rich contributions and insights. Thanks, April!

Michael Lodahl
San Gerardo, Costa Rica
Semana Santa del 2014

PART I
God, Our Creator

1
RENEWAL IN THE IMAGE OF GOD

Do not lie to one another, seeing that you have
stripped off the old self with its practices
and have clothed yourselves with the new self,
which is being renewed in knowledge according to
the image of its creator.
—Col. 3:9-10

You know that the great end of religion is
to renew our hearts in the image of God. . . .
You know that all religion which does not answer this end,
all that stops short of this, the renewal of our soul in the image of
God, after the likeness of him that created it,
is no other than a poor farce and a mere mockery of God.
—John Wesley, "Original Sin"

THIS BOOK will explore the biblical and Christian teaching that human beings are created in the image of God. It will also explore the New Testament proclamation that Jesus Christ *is* the image of God—and that we human beings, having fallen away from our calling and purpose to reflect God's character, can be renewed in the divine image through Christ.

All three of these biblical convictions are crucial to a Christian theological anthropology (i.e., teaching about what it means to be a human being, created by God and in God's image). But exploring these convictions immediately leads to a bevy of questions. For example, what does the phrase "image of God" actually mean, or even imply, in the relatively rare biblical passages in which it appears? What does "image of God" suggest about our relationship to God on the one hand, and to the rest of God's vast creation on the other? How, why, and to what extent have we humans failed in these relationships? And why is Jesus necessary to the renewal of human beings? What exactly is being renewed, and why? How does this renewal or restoration occur? Further, how ought our answers to questions like these shape our everyday behaviors in this world—a world that Scripture affirms to be God's own good creation? Indeed, every attempt to answer one question seems to lead to several more.

For all of its complexity, this idea that we are created in God's image is affirmed in both Judaism and Christianity. It is, after all, clearly stated in the opening chapter of Genesis (1:26-27). But what it actually *means* for us to be created in God's image is far less clear. The list of possible interpretations is considerably long. While along the way we certainly shall consider some of the most influential interpretations, the one we will offer in this book will focus particularly on *the human role and responsibility to protect and to nurture the world's well-being, fruitfulness, and beauty*, in the great hope that God's good creation may enjoy a viable, even rich, future. It will be important, also, that this theme be explored in the light of the New Testament proclamation that Jesus Christ is the image of God (2 Cor. 4:4; Col. 1:15; Heb. 1:3).

Even as we affirm the teaching that we humans are created in the image of God—or, as we shall explore later, that we are created *to* "image" God—it is tragically obvious that we have distorted, marred, or perhaps even entirely effaced this image through resistance against our Maker. If Jesus Christ is truly *the* image of God, it becomes all the more evident that the rest of us fall short. Differing traditions within Christianity (to say nothing of Judaism) have disagreed about the extent to which the disintegrating power of sin has damaged human existence and thus compromised the human vocation to be the image of God. Nonetheless, it is a central and universal teaching of the Christian faith that we all stand in deep need of reconciliation, redemption, and renewal. Jesus is the very embodiment of our renewal in the image of God (Eph. 4:20-24).

If Christianity aims for such a renewal of human lives—or, in John Wesley's famous words, if "the great end of religion is to renew our hearts in the image of God"—then surely it is important for us to try to comprehend what "the image of God" actually entails. Even as we insist repeatedly that in Christian Scripture and tradition Jesus Christ is identified as "the image of God," this still begs the question of how we ought to interpret the teaching of Genesis 1 regarding our calling. We seek "the light of the knowledge of the glory of God in the face of Jesus Christ" (2 Cor. 4:6) to enlighten our understanding of the biblical idea of humanity created in the divine image. We will attempt to interpret Genesis 1 in that light, but we must nonetheless do the work of interpreting Genesis 1.

Created in the Image of God

What does Genesis mean in its teaching us that human beings, male and female, are created in the image of God? Presumably, the more light that can be shed on that question, the better we will also comprehend what it means to be *renewed* in God's image. In this opening chapter we will attempt to understand "the image of God" by interpreting it within the context of the creation story of Genesis 1 as a whole.[1] Allow us to explain. Too often in Christian tradition, unfortunately, readers have cited the language of "the image of God" as though it were an abstract principle, unrelated to its immediate (to say nothing of its larger) scriptural context. Once the phrase "in the image of God" is unloosed from the narrative of Genesis 1, it becomes terribly convenient to import one's own presuppositions about what "in the image of God" must mean. Granted, all reading involves interpretation and all interpretation involves presuppositions and prior commitments. We cannot avoid these realities. Acknowledging this, we will nonetheless attempt to soften the problem by trying to interpret Genesis's teaching about human beings within its immediate context, the first creation story (1:1—2:4).

One of the initial benefits of such an approach is that it helps keep our ideas about humanity in the image of God strongly connected to the reality with which Genesis 1 is concerned: this world in which we live. Too often the popular assumption is that Christianity is not really concerned with this earth upon which we human beings live and depend, nor with the atmosphere above us from which we receive our breath and our warmth. And yet, of course, that is precisely what "the heavens and the earth" are in Genesis 1:1—the very first verse in Jewish and Christian Scripture. Our Bible—thanks to the Jewish tradition's ancient, divinely guided wisdom—begins not in some other world, some far-off spiritual realm of angels and demons, but with the creation of this material world of trees and seas, light and night, moon and monsoon, fish and fowl, whales and quails. Further, the Creator repeatedly offers a highly positive evaluation of what is coming into being: over and over, "God saw that it was good." Indeed, that little phrase is announced six times before human beings have even made their appearance in this story of creation. God sees that creation is good prior to—and thus quite apart from—the creation of *adam*, humankind.

The goodness and integrity of creation, entirely apart from human presence and activity, is not only a theme in Genesis 1 but also a truth approachable by the sciences. Many people are surprised to find that interactions between living organisms and the environment allow earth's natural ecosystems to function quite well without human involvement (and in many cases much better without human involvement). It is the interactions between living organisms and the environment that allow matter and energy to flow and sustain life.

For example, just as water cycles through living organisms and the environment, biological processes are the mechanisms through which various elements like carbon and nitrogen cycle in nature. Photosynthesis transforms the energy from the sun into carbohydrates (such as carrots, lettuce, and tomatoes), and it is these carbohydrates that provide energy for almost all of the other living organisms on earth. Other biological processes, including cellular respiration and decomposition, also facilitate the cycling of elements through an ecosystem. This flow of energy and elements sustains the community of organisms that live in an ecosystem, all quite apart from the involvement of humans. While human agricultural practices such as irrigation and fertilization have made significant progress in recent decades, our interaction often results in a change in the environment, altering the functioning of any one of these core ecosystem processes and thereby changing the functioning of the others, since they are all interconnected aspects of the same system. It is increasingly incumbent upon us human beings to be aware of the differences our presence and activities make; indeed, we shall argue that developing such awareness—and acting accordingly—is an important dimension of what it means to be created in God's image.

Reading Genesis 1 Theologically

Before proceeding further, it should be mentioned that our purpose in engaging the text of Genesis 1 is not to glean scientific information about the universe or human beings. We hope in the process to offer reasons for why this is the case.[2] But we can state at the outset that we respect the purposes of both the Holy Scriptures and the natural sciences far too much to allow them to become confused with each other. Rather than reading the text for scientific information, we will undertake this reading of Genesis 1 with hopes of gaining a richer *theological* understanding of the world in which we live, and of ourselves within it. Our guiding question is, What does it mean to be created in God's image? That is a theological question, not a scientific one. Our assumption is that Genesis 1 is a critical text for addressing this theological question.

We first read that the world we inhabit has a Creator, identified as God (Heb., *elohim*). In the beginning of God's act of creating, the "earth" or "land" (*ha'arets*) was formless and empty. It was not functioning yet as a place for life and growth. Indeed, the land could not yet be seen—only the (sur)face of "the waters" or "the deep." All was dark, deep, formless: chaotic, unpredictable waters. Yet even here there is one significant note of hope: the *ruach* of God hovered or stirred over the face of the deep waters. *Ruach* can mean breath, wind, breeze, or spirit. It is what we and many other living creatures breathe in order to live. Our first impulse might be a desire to distinguish between *ruach* as wind and *ruach* as spirit, especially God's Spirit. But this is exceedingly difficult to do, and probably impossible; throughout the Scriptures *ruach* denotes God's own life-bestowing breath, God's Spirit of life. A striking example of this idea is found in Psalm 104, a remarkably apt poem to accompany Genesis 1, that great "Hymn of Creation"[3]:

> These all [creatures of sea, sky, and land] look to you
>> to give them their food in due season;
> when you give to them, they gather it up;
>> when you open your hand, they are filled with good things.
> When you hide your face, they are dismayed;
>> when you take away their breath [*ruach*], they die and
>>> return to their dust.
> When you send forth your spirit [*ruach*], they are created;
>> and you renew the face of the ground. (Ps. 104:27-30)

The salient point here is that it would be misleading to make an overly tidy distinction between "naturalistic" and "supernaturalistic" interpretations of *ruach*. For the Scriptures, God's "breath" animates all that lives and breathes. This seems to be reflected well in the description of the Holy Spirit as "the Lord, the Giver of life" in the Nicene Creed (381 version). To read of God's *ruach*, God's breath-wind-spirit, blowing or hovering over the face of the formless deep is to encounter, at the very beginning, a subtle but hopeful promise of life and creativity to come. Accordingly, the divine *ruach* consistently bespeaks hope in the midst of hopelessness, life in the face of death, new possibilities where none could be imagined (cf. Ezek. 37). In the very opening of our Bible, then, we are struck by a great expectation that the *ruach* of God is brooding over new possibilities even in the face of the chaotic darkness of the deep.

Beyond the hopeful presence of God's "wind" or "spirit" breathing the possibilities of life, the first step the Creator takes to address the dark, chaotic waters is to call forth light. "And God saw that the light was good" (Gen. 1:4). It should be noted that the darkness is not described as "not good"—let alone as evil—but only that the light *is* good (Heb., *tov*). Where there was in the beginning only undifferentiated, chaotic, dark churning waters, now there is a distinction made by God between light/day and darkness/night. But as many other readers have observed, there is no sun. Yet "there was evening and there was morning, the first day" (1:5). The very least we can say at this point is that this "first day" of creation is not a typical day as we now understand a day: this is not planet earth making a twenty-four-hour rotation in relationship to the star we call the sun.

Next, the Creator begins to address the problem of all that water. As light was separated from darkness, so now a "dome" or "vault" (Heb., *raqia*, something stamped down or flattened) is created that will separate waters from waters—above and below. This is the work of the "second day"—again, of course, with no sun yet in the picture. This water-separating dome is the sky, with vast amounts of water above and below. This cosmology was rooted in everyday observation of the world: the waters of the Mediterranean, for instance, were a blue that closely matched the blue of the sky above. Further, water fell from that sky above, so it was reasonable for people of the time to assume that there was a very large (perhaps virtually infinite) storage of water above, held in check by the sky-roof. When the water is let through in small amounts, it is beneficial as rain; however, as we will explore further in chapter 3, the Creator will later open the "windows of the heavens" so widely that the work of the second day is virtually undone (cf. Gen. 7:11).

It is safe (and correct!) to assume that this notion of the sky above us as a kind of domed ceiling holding back a gigantic body of chaotic waters, the vestiges of a primeval act of creation, is not what we now understand to be the case, scientifically speaking. In other words, this is not how we picture the world.[4] If we seek answers in Genesis to scientific questions about the earth and its atmosphere, we seek in vain. Granted, it is believed by at least some "creationists" that Genesis 1 describes the original composition of the earth and its sky-dome sealing off these primordial waters—a composition, they would argue, that was forever changed by the great flood in the time of Noah. Unfortunately for this line of argument, it is clear that the Bible generally continues to assume this watery cosmology not only as the world's original state but as its present condition. So, for example, Psalm 104 (written well after the presumed time of Noah) praises God, "You stretch out the heavens like a tent, you set the beams of your chambers on the waters" (vv. 2-3)—and it is clear that these are the waters believed by the psalmist still to be looming and churning beyond the heavens.

On the next day, the third, God now addresses the waters below the sky-dome. Those waters are rolled back so that land may appear. The land, apparently, is assumed to have been submerged beneath all this water. With each creative step, the Creator moves creation from chaotic formlessness toward increasing order and structure. The waters that are gathered back—separated, we could say, from the land—are the "seas." This rolling back of the waters is a prominent motif in biblical pronouncements about creation. God the Creator "set a boundary that [the waters] may not pass, so that they might not again cover the earth" (Ps. 104:9). We encounter this theme again, for example, when the divine Voice proclaims to Job from the whirlwind, "[I] said [to the deep waters], 'Thus far shall you come, and no farther, and here shall your proud waves be stopped'" (38:11). God, we might say, holds the waters at bay.

It is important to note, once again, that this description of God's creative labor need not, and should not, be understood to conflict or compete with contemporary scientific understanding. For ancient peoples near the Mediterranean, biblical passages like these probably helped to explain "why the sea comes up to the shore and no further"—which was experienced as a happy arrangement, undoubtedly! Today we would probably understand this in terms of phenomena such as ocean tides (which in turn behave in relationship to the moon's gravitational pull), wind and ocean currents, and the plate tectonics of the earth's crust. While we certainly can understand these physical phenomena and relationships theologically as important elements of God's creation, there would be no reason to assume that a theological understanding of creation would eliminate the need for, or an appreciation for, the hard work of scientific description.

It is apparent that Middle Eastern peoples assumed, naturally, that the waters "gathered together into one place" (Gen. 1:9) flowed also beneath the land. This notion would readily account for underground springs that created streams or oases. The water believed to be above the sky-dome *is* the water of the (Mediterranean) sea, which *is* the water beneath the land, because it is all that primeval water that God the Creator separated into "above" and "below" and holds in place. Thus, as Genesis puts it in the story of Noah, it is not only heaven's windows that are opened but "the fountains of the great deep burst forth" (7:11)—and this can only be the same as "the deep" of Genesis 1:2.

With the appearance of land, there is now a place for vegetation. The Creator invites, "Let the earth put forth vegetation" (1:11), and the earth's response is seen by God to be good. The language and imagery of Genesis repeatedly portrays God as One whose Word calls to the world to offer its own God-given creativity back to the Creator. It is a tantalizing possibility that the Hebrew text uses a play on words to illustrate, and virtually embody, this co-creative labor: the earth is called upon by God to *tadshe deshe* ("put forth vegetation"). An English parallel might be to say that the earth is called upon to produce produce or to implant itself with plants. The created realm is invited to contribute its divinely gifted, distinctive capacities to God's creative labor; indeed, God's creative power is expressed precisely in this empowering invitation to the earth. The issue here is not to press a scientific point. The issue is a theological one regarding the nature of God's creativity: God has no need to undo or negate the creatures but is in fact pleased to co-labor with them.

We should note, by the way, that the plants and trees are sprouting without the benefit of sunlight—enough of a problem for a strictly literal interpretation of the text, but a real problem for the day-age interpretation of Genesis 1.[5]

A lovely symmetry begins to emerge with the fourth day. We recall that on the *first* day God called forth light and separated that light from darkness. On the *fourth* day, correspondingly, the actual, visible lights in our sky are called forth "to separate the day from the night" (1:14). We recall that "day" and "night" were said to have been created on the first day, so they already exist in some sense; but now, the "greater light" and the "lesser light" will function to separate day and night from one another. Today, of course, we do not think of night and day as having existence independently of our planet's relationship to the sun; in other words, rather than "separating" day and night, the sun in its relationship to our planet is what *makes* what we call "day" and "night."

More importantly, scholars suspect considerable significance in Genesis's usage of the terms "greater light" (Heb.) and "lesser light" (Heb.) instead of "sun" and "moon." In Gerhard von Rad's words, "These created objects are expressly not named 'sun' and 'moon' so that every tempting association may be evaded, for the common Semitic word for 'sun' was also a divine name."[6] In other words, Genesis discourages any tendency to identify these two prominent heavenly bodies as deities; they are only "lights," a lesser and a great-er, that have been created by God along with everything else. This is an important consideration, for it suggests the possibility that a fundamental purpose of this creation story is to discourage idola-try—the human tendency to worship various elements within the creation rather than the Creator of it all (cf. Rom. 1:18-25).

It is noteworthy, too, that the Creator announces another func-tion for these lights: "for signs and for seasons and for days and years" (Gen. 1:14). To put it simply, Genesis here suggests that the reason for the sun and the moon is to help human beings keep track of what day and month it is. While it is certainly true that our ancestors learned long ago to track the seasons and such by observing the signs in the skies, it hardly seems reasonable to assume that this is why the sun and the moon exist. It is true that their movements across the sky in relation to human observers, especially the various phases of the moon during any given month, have become markers of time's passage; this is a function of the heavenly bodies that has emerged as a result of long and careful human observation. It would hardly do, though, to say that this is why God created the sun and the moon.

Let us pursue this line of inquiry a little further. We read in verse 16 that "God made the two great lights—the greater light to rule the day and the lesser light to rule the night—and the stars." Had this verse said something like, "And the great light is itself a star, but just much closer to us human observers," this would have been a remark-able bit of scientific information. Or if it had said, "And the lesser light is not itself truly a light, but only reflects the light shone upon it by the greater light," this too would have been a rather surprising scientific detail. But of course Genesis 1 does not offer scientific data such as this, nor ought we to expect that it should. The purpose of Genesis 1 is to put those lights in their place: they are not deities to be worshipped but simply elements in God's good creation "to rule over the day and over the night, and to separate the light from the darkness" (v. 18).

The symmetry of Genesis 1 continues: as the second day provides the stage for separating the waters into "above" and "below" by the creation of a sky-dome, so now, during the fifth day, the waters below are invited by God to *yishretsu sheres*—perhaps another Hebraic play on words that finds a rough equivalent in "swarm with swarms of swimmers"—and birds are called forth to fly up there above us (but, of course, beneath the dome). In other words, the living spaces that were created by God's imposition of the sky-dome now become inhabited with creatures appropriate to each space. It is important, too, that among the "swarms of living creatures" of the waters (v. 20), "God created the great sea monsters" (v. 21). These "sea monsters" (Heb., *tannin*) were an ancient symbol, a scary personification, of "the deep"—those primeval, threatening dark waters. Where it might be natural and even expected that people would fear these mysterious monsters of the great unknown—or perhaps even offer them a kind of fearful worship—Genesis 1 calmly proclaims that they, too, are simply good creatures of the good Creator (cf. Ps. 104:25-26).

Even as we move ever nearer to the creation of human beings, it is critical to note that in this creation story God speaks to nonhuman creatures before humanity exists. "God blessed [the creatures of sky and sea, including the sea monsters], saying, 'Be fruitful and multiply and fill the waters in the seas, and let birds multiply on the earth'" (Gen. 1:22). All of God's creatures are blessed by their Creator to thrive, to produce generations of offspring far beyond themselves.

We remember that on the third day the waters below were rolled back so that dry land might appear, providing a place for plants and trees to grow. Following the symmetrical arrangements of the chapter, now the Creator invites the land on the sixth day to "bring forth living creatures of every kind: cattle and creeping things and wild animals of the [land]" (v. 24). The plant life called into being on the third day will provide nourishment for these earthen creatures of the sixth day.

The Image of God as a Divine Calling

Surely it is noteworthy that the creation of *adam*—the Hebrew word for "human," "humanity," "humankind," or "human beings"— also occurs on the sixth day. Perhaps contrary to our expectations and prejudices, there is no special day set aside uniquely for the creation of human beings, male and female. Indeed, since the term *adam* derives directly from the Hebrew term for ground, *adamah*, it makes all the more sense that humanity is created with the rest of the land animals on the sixth day. This is a theological commentary on human existence, the rudimentary beginnings of a theological anthropology, that roots us deeply in earth with all of our fellow creatures. "You [shall] return to the ground [Heb., *adamah*], for out of it you were taken; you are dust, and to dust you shall return" (Gen. 3:19).

On the other hand, it is obvious that Genesis describes human beings as unique among God's earthy creatures in certain important ways. One obvious hint of this lies in the fascinating shift in the nature of God's speech: from "Let there be" and even "Let the earth bring forth" to "*Let us* make humankind in *our* image, according to *our* likeness" (1:3, 6, 11, 14, 24, 26). We will attempt to explore this fascinating shift in divine language in the following chapter; for now, we will simply begin to attempt to unpack this mysterious statement, "So God created humankind [again, *adam*] in his image" (1:27).

Critical to the overall argument of this book is that, while what precisely defines "the image of God" is not described in the passage, there is definitely a particular function that is assigned to this creature, *adam*. This should not surprise us. We have already seen repeatedly in Genesis 1 that the elements of creation have been described in what might be called functional terms, that is, in terms of how things (are supposed to) work in relationship to other things.[7]

Generally speaking, the Scriptures are far more interested in describing how things and people (and even God) function—how they act and interact—than in offering precise descriptions of their nature or definitions of their essence. So, to return to the Genesis depiction of humanity's creation, we find no attempt to define "the image of God" in terms of a set of abilities or capacities that are stipulated to be unique to human beings. Genesis 1's description of humanity's creation includes no mention of reason, freedom, creativity, imagination, capacity for language, and so forth—the sorts of capacities that have often been listed among the leading human attributes explored in the history of Christian interpretation. Instead, in Genesis 1 we encounter a description of function, a divine calling or task for which we human beings are assumed to be suited.

Of course, our function may very well depend upon our possessing certain features or capacities. What a being is able to *do* usually will depend strongly upon what a being *is*. So in this instance, this human role, given by God, to "fill the earth and subdue it; and have dominion" over earth's creatures does inevitably imply that we must exercise certain critical abilities. Perhaps the list of abilities will not differ much, if at all, from the list offered in the previous paragraph. Nonetheless, the point would be that Scripture does not identify as "the image of God" these or any other capacities supposedly unique to human beings; instead, "the image of God" is simply described in terms of this calling to "subdue" and "have dominion." Indeed, the recurring temptation in interpreting this passage is to identify some set of abilities as the image of God, and then invert the biblical language to talk about "the image of God in humanity." The simple fact, however, is that "the image of God" is never described in the Bible as some power or attribute or capacity "in" us; instead, we are created *in God's image*. And that is immediately described in functional terms.

Psalm 8 provides a wonderful angle on this very idea. While the phrase "image of God" is not employed—the phrase is, after all, exceedingly rare in the Bible, a point that should give us pause—the psalmist does ask God the perennial question, "What are human beings [*adam*] that you are mindful of them, mortals [*ben adam*, or the offspring of humanity] that you care for them?" (v. 4). The query is posed in the light, we might say, of "the moon and the stars" (v. 3); given the vast expanse of "your heavens" (v. 3), how can you, O God, really take notice of us puny human creatures on earth?

This question packs a much heavier punch now than it could ever have in the time of David. While certainly the night sky reveals an overwhelming expanse of stars—once you escape the big city!—the facts that lie beyond the observation of our naked eye are utterly astounding. We now understand that our planet revolves around a medium-sized star that is one of many billions of similar stars within our Milky Way galaxy alone. Traveling at the speed of light, it would take about ten thousand years to traverse just this one galaxy. Beyond our Milky Way, astronomers estimate that there are billions more galaxies, each with billions of stars, some of unimaginable magnitude. Surely it is literally the case that our minds cannot comprehend these numbers, nor the possible size of the universe. Meanwhile, back on our grain-of-sand planet Earth, we ask again with the psalmist: "What are human beings that you are mindful of them?" (v. 4).

The reply is astonishing. "Yet you have made them a little lower than God [the Hebrew term here is *elohim*, the same one used throughout Gen. 1 for God], and crowned them with glory and honor" (v. 5). This Hebrew song of praise to God does not shy away from a shockingly high estimation of God's creature, *adam*. We should note, accordingly, that God's glory is not compromised or lessened by human greatness, for indeed it is God who has "crowned [us] with glory and honor." What sort of God, what kind of Creator, is this? Further, what can it possibly mean that God has made human beings "a little lower than God"?

The answer lies, we propose, in the functional description that immediately follows in verses 6-9:

You have given them dominion over the works of your hands;

you have put all things under their feet,

all sheep and oxen,

and also the beasts of the field,

the birds of the air, and the fish of the sea,

whatever passes along the paths of the sea.

O LORD, our Sovereign,

how majestic is your name in all the earth!

It appears that God's majesty "in all the earth" is to be reflected—it is to be re-presented or *imaged*—throughout earthly creation by humans who otherwise very easily might feel small and insignificant in the face of this unspeakably vast universe. In other words, as in Genesis 1 we read that *adam* is created in God's image, so in Psalm 8 we find that humanity's "glory and honor" lies in a God-granted task to exercise "dominion over the works of [God's] hands." Our Creator calls us to a task, entrusting us to be those creatures whose lives willingly magnify the divine majesty on this planet. This is what it means to be "made a little lower than God." It is not an ontological [Gk., *ontos,* "being"] description of our inner essence as lying only a few degrees below the divine nature. Scripture repeatedly reminds us that we humans are no more than creatures of dust, feeble and frail. Instead, we are "a little lower than God" simply, and precisely, in terms of the godly task assigned to us: we are created and called to *function* as God's representatives. It is critical to note that this psalm was penned well into human history; *adam* is, at the time of its writing, deeply entrenched in the powerful reality of sin. But nothing in this psalm even hints that human sin—our constant falling short of the calling to which we are called—has discouraged God from continuing to create us to be the divine image, crowning us with glory and honor. This is nothing short of miraculous.

There is one other biblical illustration of this notion of humanity *functioning* as God's representative that we hope will drive the idea home as we bring this chapter to a close. It is the story of the calling of Moses to lead the people of Israel out of Egypt (Exod. 3:1—4:17). First, we should note the somewhat surprising desire of God that a human agent even be necessary to Israel's liberation: "The cry of the Israelites has now come to me; I have also seen how the Egyptians oppress them. So come, I will send you to Pharaoh to bring my people, the Israelites, out of Egypt" (3:9-10). Surely the Creator of the heavens and the earth can accomplish this liberation apart from any human agent; and yet, we encounter again the mystery of a Creator who intends to accomplish the divine purposes by way of a representative. God even respects Moses's ability to raise objections, ask questions, throw up roadblocks, and invent excuses, patiently dealing with Moses's dodges one by one (3:11—4:13).

Finally, however, the text narrates that God's holy anger burned against Moses. We might expect Moses to be reduced to ashes. Instead, the Voice from the burning bush next patiently proposes,

> What of your brother Aaron, the Levite? I know that he can speak fluently; even now he is coming out to meet you, and when he sees you his heart will be glad. You shall speak to him and put the words in his mouth; and I will be with your mouth and with his mouth, and will teach you what you shall do. He indeed shall speak for you to the people; he shall serve as a mouth for you, and you shall serve as God for him. Take in your hand this staff, with which you shall perform the signs. (4:14-17)

How is it that God, Creator of the universe, can be so humble as to enter into conversation with Moses, and finally even offer a compromise with Moses? The Voice from the burning bush agrees to alter the plan for redeeming Israel to include Moses's brother Aaron in this mighty work of redemption. Most critically for our purposes, we note that the Voice proclaims that as Aaron will serve as a mouth for Moses, Moses will serve as God for Aaron. This is striking language, and it means that Moses will *function* as God, will *represent* God, to Aaron. Of course, this is essentially what God has been trying to get Moses to do all along: to *function for God*, to *represent God*, to the people of Israel and even to their Egyptian oppressors, and especially to Pharaoh.

This description of Moses, then, is simply a special case of the idea we have been exploring from Genesis 1 regarding the creation of human beings. Our Creator makes all of humanity—every human being, and particularly all human beings together precisely in their sociality—"a little lower than God" in their function as God's representatives. This is what we are made for. It is a high and holy calling, one "crowned with glory and honor." Indeed, it may seem overwhelming, too tall an order. The human family has often shown a distinct resistance to such a demanding vocation. The argument of the chapters that follow is that, despite our resistance and rebellion, God is persistent and patient, laboring painstakingly for humanity's renewal in the image of God through Jesus Christ. And if it is truly a renewal, then it is not a rescinding or denial of this calling we encounter in Genesis 1; indeed, in Paul's words, "the gifts and the calling of God are irrevocable" (Rom. 11:29). Genesis 1, then, must still be in effect. Before we delve further into the attempt to understand the nature of this calling, this vocation, it will be helpful, and probably necessary, to probe the question of who this God is who has created and called us for such a purpose.

2
IN THE IMAGE OF
THE SOCIAL GOD

I ask . . . that they may all be one. As you, Father,
are in me and I am in you, may they also be in us,
so that the world may believe that you have sent me.
—John 17:20-21

With an honest openness of mind, let us always remember
the kindred between man and man; and cultivate
that happy instinct whereby, in the original constitution
of our nature, God has strongly bound us to each other.
—John Wesley, *Notes on the New Testament*

AS WE mentioned briefly in the previous chapter, while still in the sixth day of the Genesis 1 story the reader suddenly encounters a new style of divine discourse. It is no longer "Let there be" or even "Let the earth bring forth." It is, instead, "*Let us* make humankind [*adam*] in our image, according to our likeness" (1:26). It seems that we find here a more careful, perhaps a more self-reflective, act on God's part. Further, we encounter the somewhat baffling plural pronouns in God's self-reflective activity. What shall we make of the "Let us"?

There are several directions we could take to address this important question. It is true, even if mildly troubling, that the Hebrew term *elohim* found throughout Genesis 1, virtually always translated as "God," is a plural form; thus it can, in literal terms, be translated "gods."[1] But the Hebrew verb forms in Genesis 1 are singular rather than plural, as are most of the other divine pronouns throughout the chapter. Further, the confession of the people of Israel—that *God is One* (Deut. 6:4; Mark 12:32)—is also the confession of the Christian church universal. It seems of potential significance, then, that it is precisely at this point in the creation narrative, when its subject is the creation of *adam* as male and female in the image of God, that we encounter "Let *us*" and "in *our* image."

While it would be hasty and unwarranted to assume a full-blown Trinitarian teaching in these verses, we might nonetheless venture cautiously in that direction. We could at least say that the text seems to gesture toward some kind of sociality in God's being, vague and unformed as that gesture might be. God is One, and yet God may also speak forth in a "plural" voice. (*Let us . . .*) Again, given that *adam* is a singular reality ("humankind") yet also a plural reality ("male and female"), perhaps we can suggest that the communal richness of God's being is best reflected in our human plurality and diversity when we commit to loving and cooperating with one another. If this is so, then the Creator intends for the rich diversity of the human race to represent (or "re-present") God within the creaturely realm. This would mean that the human task, as we described it in the first chapter of this book, is meant to be fulfilled together, as a social responsibility of human beings everywhere and at all times.

Divine Wisdom, Divine Word

The prologue to the gospel of John (1:1-18) in the New Testament overtly offers a reading of Genesis 1 that contributes to our attempts to interpret the plural voice in *Let us*. "In the beginning was the Word [Gk., *logos*], and the Word was with God, and the

Word was God."[2] God is the Creator, to be sure, but "all things came into being through [the Word], and without [the Word] not one thing came into being" (John 1:3). What is this Word, this Logos? Most simply, it is God's Speech, God's eternal Communication. The notion of the Logos implies that in God's very nature is the distinct disposition toward messaging, toward communication and communing. God reaches out in Speech, in Word. The Jewish people would come to identify this Word also with divine Wisdom, perhaps most famously and obviously in Proverbs 8:

Does not wisdom call,
    and does not understanding raise her voice? . . .
"To you, O people, I call,
    and my cry is to all that live. . . .
I walk in the way of righteousness,
    along the paths of justice,
endowing with wealth those who love me,
    and filling their treasuries.
The LORD created me at the beginning of his work,
    the first of his acts of long ago.
Ages ago I was set up,
    at the first, before the beginning of the earth.
When there were no depths I was brought forth,
    when there were no springs abounding with water.
Before the mountains had been shaped,
    before the hills, I was brought forth—
when he had not yet made earth and fields,
    or the world's first bits of soil.
When he established the heavens, I was there,
    when he drew a circle on the face of the deep,
when he made firm the skies above,
    when he established the fountains of the deep,
when he assigned to the sea its limit,
    so that the waters might not transgress his command,

when he marked out the foundations of the earth,

then I was beside him, like a master worker;

and I was daily his delight,

rejoicing before him always,

rejoicing in his inhabited world

and delighting in the human race.

And now, my children, listen to me:

happy are those who keep my ways. (Vv. 1, 4, 20-32)

In this well-known passage, Divine Wisdom is personified as a woman who freely offers guidance to human beings, all of whom sorely need it. Proverbs 8 seems to suggest that the "Let us" and "in our image" language of Genesis 1 is most wisely understood to signify God *and* this personification of Divine Wisdom, sometimes referred to by scholars as Lady Wisdom. God's Word *is* Wisdom, and God's Wisdom *is* the creative communication and communing of the Word. In some truly indescribable way, this Wisdom was coming to be understood as a reality that is, at least in some important respects, distinct from God, alongside God—and yet also sharing in God's own being and nature.[3] "I [i.e., Wisdom] was beside [God], like a master worker; and I was daily his delight, rejoicing before him always, rejoicing in his inhabited world and delighting in the human race" (Prov. 8:30-31). The created world apparently flows joyously forth from this fruitful friendship, this kinship, between God and Wisdom/Word.

Though this Wisdom/Word is often personified as a human, and a woman in particular, it is important to remember that it is not in actuality a human being until the point of the incarnation: "And the Word became flesh and lived among us . . . full of grace and truth. . . . The law indeed was given through Moses; grace and truth came through Jesus Christ" (John 1:14, 17). There is no question that passages like Proverbs 8 helped to pave the way for the early church's conviction that the divine Word, active in the creation of all things, actually entered into the world as a human being, Jesus of Nazareth

(Matt. 11:28-30; 1 Cor. 1:23-25; Col. 2:2-3). Later in the gospel of John this Word become flesh prays, "Father, glorify me in your own presence with the glory that I had in your presence before the world existed" (17:5); here it becomes obvious (if it wasn't before) that we are being directed to interpret the language of Genesis 1:26, "Let us make [adam] in our image, according to our likeness," as a kind of "conversation" between God and the Word/Wisdom of God, existing somehow alongside of God.

If we confess and believe that "the Word became flesh and lived among us" (John 1:14) in the historical person of Jesus, then his life and mission should be of crucial importance for how we interpret Genesis 1. If the Word that God speaks in the labor of creation—*Let there be; Let us make*—has become a human being in the miracle of incarnation, then that divine speech, as well as its creative intention, must ultimately and fundamentally be heard through the gospel of Jesus Christ. Simply put, we are to read the words of Genesis 1 in the glorious light of the Word who became flesh and lived among us. Jesus Christ is the full flowering, the final revelation, of the creative Word we hear in the creation story of Genesis 1. To employ the final verse of John's prologue, "No one has ever seen God" the Creator; no one has adequately, let alone entirely, grasped or comprehended who God is or what God is like. However, "It is God the only Son, who is close to the Father's heart, who has made God known" to us (John 1:18). God the Creator is made known to us through the words and works of Jesus, God's Beloved (14:8-11). This inference ought to exercise considerable influence in our interpretation of Genesis 1 as a testimony about God the Creator.

If the "Let us" of Genesis 1 is indeed best understood as signifying the relation between God and God's Word, then for Christian faith that relation has become revealed and realized in time and place through the incarnation of the Word. In the light of that assumption, we turn to Jesus's High Priestly Prayer in John 17 to illuminate further our call to function as God's image. "As you, Father, are in me and I am in you, may they also be in us. . . . The glory that you have given me I have given them, so that they may be one, as we are one, I in them and you in me, so that they may become completely one" (vv. 21-23). This "glory" God has given Jesus, a glory that Jesus in turn shares with his followers, is explicitly described as a glory "which you have given me because you loved me before the foundation of the world" (v. 24). Thus, in Jesus's fellowship of disciples there is a kind of fulfillment of God's intention for humanity as described in Genesis 1:26; the incarnate Word provides the opening ("I am the door" [John 10:9, REB]) through which humans may return to the kind of divinely constituted communion for which we have been created. And that communion, that fellowship, is intended by the Creator to image or reflect God within the world. Earlier we suggested that humanity as "male and female"—that is, as plural, diverse, and social—is created to function as God's image. In the light of the incarnation, we can now posit that the basis for human beings functioning as God's image is grounded in the intimate, loving, and revealing relationship between God and the Word, or between the Father and the Son, as proclaimed especially in John's gospel.

It is fascinating that we read in 1 John 4:12, "No one has ever seen God"—precisely the same stark claim that we encounter in John 1:18. In neither instance is this statement simply about God's invisibility; rather, it is proclaiming the infinite mystery and utter transcendence of God. In the gospel of John, this strong statement is followed by the good news that the Divine Mystery has been "made known" to us by "the only Son, who is close to the Father's heart" (1:18). In other words, the profound challenge of knowing the Infinite Mystery is resolved in the person, words, and deeds of Jesus. In 1 John, however, this identical statement, "No one has ever seen God," is given a different reply: "If we love one another, God lives in our midst, and God's love is perfected in our midst" (4:12, author's translation). Or we might translate that final clause, "and God's love reaches its fulfillment in our midst." When and if we love another as God has loved us (cf. 3:16-17), God's purpose in having created human beings actually is fulfilled—for "God is love" (4:8, 16) and we have been created to "image" or reflect this God who is "Love Divine, all loves excelling."[4]

The Inviting Word of Creation and the Word that Became Flesh

The foregoing reflections certainly ought to influence the way we interpret Genesis 1's description of our human calling as creatures in the image of God. Biblical scholars tend to understand the language of "image" in Genesis 1:26-28 as a creative adaptation of a practice common among earthly rulers during the era in which the creation story was being composed. Such rulers were known to have "images" or statues of themselves erected in the farther reaches of their empires, essentially as substantial reminders of their rule or authority to their distant subjects.[5] Assuming the validity of the idea that Genesis 1 draws upon such political practices in order to proclaim the human vocation or calling within the creaturely realm, we are provided a graphic reply to the perennial human question, "Why do I exist?" As we have argued in the previous chapter, humans exist, essentially, to be God's representatives in God's good creation. Or, better yet, we are created to live and labor *together*, "male and female," as social, relational, interdependent creatures—and thus to "image" God, whom "no one has ever seen," in the fundamental reality of our communal existence. We are here to represent or "image" God to one another, certainly; but as far as Genesis 1 is concerned, the more fundamental role is our imaging or representation of God to the rest of creation, to all of its nonhuman creatures. In Gerhard von Rad's words, "The decisive thing about man's similarity to God, therefore, is his function in the nonhuman world."[6]

If the human calling is to "image" or represent God, the obvious question is, What is God like? What do we re-present when we represent God? As we have argued, for Christians the fundamental reply to such a question is answered in the person of Jesus Christ. Even as John warns that "no one has ever seen God" (John 1:18), so also Jesus, in the same gospel, says to Philip, "Whoever has seen me has seen the Father" (14:9)—precisely because "what God was, the Word was" (1:1, REB).

As we read the language of Genesis 1 in its description of the human vocation, we ought to—indeed, we *must*—bring this christological principle with us. For example, we read in Genesis 1:28, "Be fruitful and multiply"—and we immediately should recall that this same command has already been issued to all of the other creatures in God's good world (1:22). Hence, we may readily assume that our human multiplying ought not to be pursued at the expense of all the other creatures to whom God has already spoken the same Word. Further, that same Word became flesh and lived among us as a servant, washing his disciples' feet and even laying down his life for them (1 John 3:16). Our fruitfulness ought to be engendered with the same kind of humble, self-giving love for all of the rest of God's beloved creatures on the land and in the waters and the sky. Yet, during the past century the human population has grown exponentially, and of the seven billion people currently living on earth, about half live in poverty and at least one-fifth are severely undernourished. This human population explosion is impacting all forms of life, visible and microscopic. In fact, during this past century species are going extinct at a rate one hundred to one thousand times faster than they were previously.[7]

Granted, the language of Genesis 1 is strong: "fill the earth and subdue it; and have dominion over" all the nonhuman creatures (v. 28). The Hebrew term generally translated as "dominion" (*rada*) does suggest a kind of "treading" or "trampling" upon these other creatures. However, if we take seriously our christological lens for interpreting Genesis 1, we cannot run amok with the rhetoric of *rada*. If the Creator we are to image has been revealed in Jesus, presumably we are called to live gently and peaceably upon the earth.

As previously argued, God blessed all creatures and co-labors with them to produce generations of offspring far beyond themselves. Domination that leads to destruction contradicts this divine call to be fruitful and multiply. Indeed, the term "dominion," from the Latin *dominus* or "lord," itself takes on radically new meanings when the lord in question is Jesus of Nazareth.[8]

Exercising Dominion in the Light of Christ

We can certainly continue to take seriously the fact that the language of Genesis 1:28 has a forceful edge to it. Even when we understand human "dominion" (and the command to "fill the earth and subdue it") in the light of Jesus Christ, there is something about such language that realistically recognizes that there are elements and forces in creation that call for some kind of "taming."[9] We humans have to work hard to make a home in this world. But we are also called upon by our Creator to utilize all our intellectual and creative gifts to ensure that all of God's beloved creatures have a home in this world as well, so that they might continue to multiply. We build dwellings, cities, dams, dikes, all to help protect human survival. We also establish animal and land preserves; we labor to protect and nourish the diversity of animal species; we consider how our dietary choices affect ecosystems; we seek alternative modes of energy and agriculture; and the list goes on. Obviously we do not all devote our energies to such activities, and obviously some of these activities at times work at cross-purposes with others, even in our best intentions. It is difficult work. It requires serious thought and exertion. Perhaps we can begin to understand terms like "subdue" and "have dominion" in these ways—and that even here, especially here, the Christian faith calls us to undertake this strenuous and challenging task in ways that truly reflect the God revealed in Jesus Christ. Our argument is that this is at least an aspect, and a significant aspect, of what is entailed in our "being renewed in knowledge according to the image of [our] creator" (Col. 3:10).

We should note also that "every plant yielding seed . . . and every tree with seed in its fruit" is given to the humans to eat (Gen. 1:29). The salient point here is that being created in God's image, and being given the task of "dominion" over all the creatures, does not lead to what we might commonly have come to expect: that "dominating" or "subduing" all those creatures implies permission (let alone the right) to eat them! The point is not that we must become vegetarians; it is that we can at least contemplate the possibility and consider its possible merits. Human beings are able to weigh the arguments for a vegetarian diet—such as reducing fresh water consumption, air pollution, land degradation, energy use, deforestation, and biodiversity decline. Of all creatures on earth, so far as we know, only humans are capable of giving careful and moral attention to what we eat and why. Further, we can say at least that eating meat is not an immediate consequence or implication of being created in God's image. Again in von Rad's words, "Just as [the human creature] was created with them on the same day, so he is referred with them to the same table for his bodily needs."[10]

The vision for creation we encounter in this opening chapter of the Bible teaches us that the primary mode of relation between humanity and the more-than-human world is that of functioning as God's "image"—"mirroring" God, we might say, to all the other creatures. This function, it appears, might be reduced to two particular responsibilities: (1) to ensure and to protect the goodness of creation as repeatedly declared by the Creator; and (2) to live in such a way that God's blessing and command to all those nonhuman creatures, "Be fruitful and multiply," may actually be fulfilled.

Augustine's Rule of Interpretation

Finally, no theological engagement with Genesis 1 is complete without giving attention to the struggles of Augustine (AD 354—430) to interpret the opening passage of our Bible. In his *Confessions*, he wrestles long and hard over the question of interpreting Genesis 1, particularly in the light of several competing readings of the text in his own time. For a moment he imagines what it would be like to interview Moses as a way to settle the argument. Perhaps an audience with the author would help? Probably not, he decides: "Even if Moses were to appear to us and say, 'This is what I meant,'" writes Augustine, "we should not see his thoughts but would simply believe his word."[11] In other words, a face-to-face, oral interpretation of the Genesis text—even one given by the author himself—would not and cannot do away with the inevitable challenges of interpretation. We would not "see his thoughts," so the author's mind would remain inaccessible. We would still need to *interpret* what Moses said he meant!

Augustine responds to the unavoidable burden of interpretation by moving toward Jesus. Drawing from the words of Jesus in Matthew 22:36-40, Augustine understands "God's teaching" essentially to be that we are to love God and all neighbors. He then wisely notes Jesus's further comment that "on these two commandments hang all the law and the prophets" (v. 40). Augustine recalls that "the law" or Torah includes Genesis, and thus includes the very passages of controversy in Genesis 1 itself. To put it simply, all of Genesis 1 "hangs on" the dual commandment of love for God and neighbor. On this basis he can make a crucial appeal to his readers, especially to those who may disagree with his interpretation of Genesis 1:

Let us not, therefore, "go beyond what is laid down for us," . . . "Let us love the Lord our God with our whole heart and our whole soul and our whole mind, and our neighbour as ourselves." Whatever Moses meant in his books, unless we believe that he meant it to be understood in the spirit of these two precepts of charity, we are "treating God as a liar," for we attribute to [God's] servant thoughts at variance with [God's] teaching.[12]

A little further on in his *Confessions* Augustine asks, "Do you not see how foolish it is to enter into mischievous arguments which are an offense against that very charity for the sake of which [Moses] wrote every one of the words that we are trying to explain?"[13] We must keep in mind that Augustine is still grappling with the open-ing verses of Genesis and is suggesting that they were written "for the sake of . . . charity," for the sake of calling us to greater love for God and all neighbors. To dispute bitterly over how to understand Genesis's opening chapter, ironically, runs the great risk of missing the very purpose of the text.

Similarly, in his book *On Christian Teaching* Augustine stipulat-ed that difficult biblical passages "are to be elucidated in terms of the need to nourish love," for "scripture enjoins nothing but love"; thus, any given passage should be "interpreted according to the aim of love, whether it be love of God or love of one's neighbor, or both."[14] For Augustine, then, "God's teaching" is consistently aiming "to nourish love" in our lives and all relationships. Genesis 1 describes human beings as created in God's image, and now we have come to comprehend, through Jesus Christ, that *God is love.* Now we can see that to be created in God's image is to be created for love—to receive love, to share love. According to Augustine this love for God and all neighbors is the very point of Genesis, including Genesis 1.

Given this Augustinian hermeneutic derived from Jesus's in-structions in the gospel of Matthew, the teaching of Genesis 1 that human beings are created in God's image ought to be interpreted in the light of the dual command upon which all the Torah hangs: to be created in God's image is to be created to love God and neighbor. While this is not identical with, nor reducible to, the emphasis we have given in this chapter to the human vocation of protecting the goodness of God's creation and insuring that all creatures have the space, resources, and opportunity for self-propagation and "filling the earth," neither is it at all alien to it. We must come to know and appreciate deeply how interconnected, how interdependent, we hu-man creatures are with all of God's other beloved creatures and the environment of earth, sea, and sky that we all share. We cannot love our neighbor in some kind of environmental vacuum, in isolation from issues of sufficient food for all, breathable air, potable water, living space, and shelter.

The issue of global climate change provides a dramatic example of how inequalities in levels of wealth, education, and health status leave some people (our "neighbors"!) and communities far more vulnerable. The Intergovernmental Panel on Climate Change (IPCC) unequivocally agrees that as a result of increases in greenhouse gases the earth's temperatures are warming significantly, leading to more extreme weather and a rise in sea level. The effects of these changes are felt first, and most deeply, by the poor people of our planet, the majority of whom reside in rural areas where farming is the dominant economic activity. Further, impoverished people may spend as much as two-thirds of their income on food. A drought or severe weather event can reduce agricultural productivity and escalate food prices, impacting the health and livelihood of the locals in rural, undeveloped areas.[15]

The importance of agriculture to the poor is particularly true for a country like Tanzania (in southeastern Africa), where agriculture accounts for about half of gross production and employs about 80 percent of the labor force. Agriculture in Tanzania is also primarily rain-fed, with only 2 percent of arable land having irrigation facilities—far below the potentially irrigable share. The primary Tanzanian crop is corn, which is particularly susceptible to adverse weather events. In 2001 there were 12.3 million Tanzanians, or about 36 percent of the country's population, living below the national poverty line. Climate-induced changes in agricultural productivity will likely continue to have severe implications for the Tanzanians through price and income effects—and of course this is but one country.[16]

There is no question that Tanzanians are our neighbors. Further, Jesus in his parable of the Good Samaritan transformed the scholar's question *Who is my neighbor?* into a far more radical one: *Who proved to be a neighbor to the person in need?* (Luke 10:29, 36). After Jesus's revolutionary parable, "neighbor" can no longer refer to a category of persons outside ourselves; instead, Jesus challenges his followers to *be the neighbors*. If we actively seek to *become* the neighbor, then surely there is no one anywhere who is not my neighbor. The Tanzanian's plight demands my attention, compassion, and action because I am called to be her neighbor. But this requires that I be willing to become informed and then allow that information to make a difference in how I live every day within God's good creation.

If love for the neighbor cannot be properly or responsibly exercised in an environmental vacuum, neither can we love the neighbor in isolation from God's will that all other creatures, beyond human beings, also have opportunity to flourish. But even if we set aside for a moment such considerations, rooted in Genesis 1, regarding the well-being of God's vast plethora of living creatures, and if instead we briefly consider only the importance placed upon loving our human neighbors as ourselves, we face a sobering question: How do we live in the present moment in such a way as to love *our neighbors of the future* as we love ourselves? How shall we live now such that our lives are an expression of divine love for those creatures yet to come, human and nonhuman? Does not God love them as well?

As we continue to grow in our understanding of how our actions in the present affect profoundly the nature of the world and its resources that our children and grandchildren will inherit, surely love of neighbor becomes a guiding principle for all who understand themselves through Jesus Christ as "the new self, which is being renewed in knowledge according to the image of its creator" (Col. 3:10). If "on these two commandments [of love for God and neighbor] hang all the law and the prophets," as Matthew 22:37-39 put it and the Tanzanians' fellow African Augustine wisely read it, then surely we are to read all of Scripture with an eye toward nourishing and nurturing greater, deeper, and wider love for God and for all our neighbors. That includes our neighbors of the future with whom we share God's good creation.

And on the Seventh Day . . .

There is, of course, one more day to be considered. We shall have opportunity to discuss the critical importance of the seventh day in chapter 7, but for now we might offer this: Sabbath reminds us that God is God and we are not. Granted, the divine command to rest on the Sabbath day is grounded in God's own rest from labor (Exod. 20:8-11), so in one sense we are being "like God" when we breathe deeply and rest. But it is also a profound reminder that, for all that the Creator entrusts into humanity's care as God's image in the world, we are still only creatures. We are not the Creator. Even if God calls upon *adam* as male and female to "fill the earth and subdue it; and have dominion," we are nonetheless made on the sixth day with the other land animals; we are creatures of dust, feeble and frail, desperately needing to rest and to be reminded that this world is God's world and that it spins in God's loving, long-suffering hands.

3
AN EVERLASTING COVENANT

God said, "This is the sign of the covenant that I make
between me and you and every living creature that is with
you, for all future generations. . . . When the bow is in
the clouds, I will see it and remember the everlasting
covenant between God and every living creature of all flesh
that is on the earth."
—Gen. 9:12, 16

God had drowned the world once, and still the world is as
provoking as ever; yet he will never drown it any more,
for he deals not with us according to our sins.
—John Wesley, *Notes on the Old Testament*

AS WE CONTINUE to explore the biblical roots of the teaching
that human beings are created in God's image, we turn now to the
Genesis story of the flood. We do this precisely because Noah's story
illustrates so much of what we have argued is entailed in the idea
that humans are created in the image of God: we are called to be, in
John Wesley's words, "the channel of conveyance" between the Creator and all other creatures so that "all the blessings of God" should
"flow through [humans]"[1] to the more-than-human world. To nav-

igate the deep waters of this biblical narrative, we will again try to focus our attention upon the question of what the story of Noah suggests *theologically*: how God is portrayed, how God interacts with creation, and how human beings are called upon to participate in the divine story. Our ruling assumption, then, is that the fundamental purpose of this narrative is to communicate theological truths—the most fundamental of which, as we learned from Augustine at the conclusion of chapter 2, is that human beings have been created to love God with all of their being and to love all neighbors as themselves. Further, we will assume that love for all neighbors and care for God's creation are inextricably intertwined concerns.

A question immediately arises. Given what we have claimed in the previous chapters about God's compassionate love for all creatures, this story itself should give us pause. How could the Creator do such a thing as to flood the world? Why so much destruction? How can we begin to understand, theologically, what this story seems to suggest? In what follows, we will propose four crucial ideas to which this narrative gives rise.

Reading Noah's Narrative Theologically

First, God the Creator seems to be genuinely disappointed in the way that creation is heading. Seeing the wickedness of humanity, Genesis narrates, "The LORD was sorry that he had made humankind on the earth, and it grieved him to his heart" (6:6). This language is at least a little troubling. Sorrow and grief are not the sorts of attributes that theologians typically assign to God! How could an omniscient God, for whom the future is already, eternally and perfectly known, really be "sorry" about creating human beings? Can God "grieve" over a long foregone conclusion, an entirely unsurprising outcome? How can these things be? Further, could we not suspect God of overreacting? "I will blot out from the earth the human beings I have created—people together with animals and creeping things and birds of the air, for I am sorry that I have made them" (v. 7). Wait—*what?*

It is, of course, possible to soften this problem by suggesting that even though nothing takes the omniscient God by surprise, this language of Genesis underscores just how deeply the Creator cares for the creation. In other words, it might be argued that though God could perfectly see it all coming in timeless omniscience, the text's description of God's sorrow and grief testifies to the depths of divine love and compassion. On the other hand, it is not difficult to surmise that it is precisely compassion that is missing from this picture! Certainly, God's reaction seems extreme.

Undoubtedly, we should recognize that the passage contains elements that theologians and biblical scholars would call *anthropomorphic* (lit., "human-shaped"). God is described here in ways that seem more like a deeply disappointed human being than they do the holy, transcendent Creator of all things. Of course, all human speech about God (including the language of the Bible) is anthropomorphic to some degree, since it is we feeble and finite humans who speak and write these words. We should always acknowledge this. But here, in the Noah narrative, the anthropomorphic elements stand out so strongly, so threateningly! How do we make sense of God's initial determination that not only the human beings—who were originally intended by God to "image" or reflect the Creator within creation—but all (or at least most!) of creation should be obliterated? And if all of creation now rests under God's deep disappointment and judgment, why should all the fish and sea monsters get a free pass?

How can we understand such a rendering of God? Let us suggest that we can take this biblical passage seriously, and interpret it theologically, without reading it literally. What we mean is this: acknowledging that we think within the limitations of human language regarding the utterly transcendent Holy One, this passage certainly points us toward the real, and serious, engagement of God the Creator with the world of creation. If "sorrow" and "grief" are terms that are finally too bold, too bald-faced, for describing God's reactions to human sin and violence (v. 11), they do at least suggest to us that God dwells with creation in a way that bespeaks a deep investment. God *dwells with* creation. Perhaps God is even willing to dwell with creation's temporal nature—an idea that is already present in Genesis 1, where, as we have seen, God creates in a "timeful" and gradual way through the passage of six days.[2] To put it simply, God does not merely "blink" everything all at once into existence. So Genesis leads us to consider God's creating and sustaining labors as occurring profoundly within the processes of time. But if the world is essentially temporal, and if God truly is willing to dwell with the world as the world actually exists, then time's passage would be real to God. If God is willing, perhaps even pleased, to dwell truly with us creatures of time, then the idea that sorrow and grief could in some way be attributed to God should not so greatly dismay us. Even if the language of divine surprise or disappointment is strong, it need not be considered misleading; it testifies of the Creator's true and real engagement with creation.

Second, just as God did not simply or timelessly "blink" the heavens and the earth into existence, so now, even in the face of the world's great evils, *God does not "blink" in a new world to replace the old*. This merits careful consideration. The way that theologians have sometimes discussed divine omnipotence, it would seem natural to suppose that God could have simply wiped clean the divine mental slate and popped a new and improved world immediately into being. How hard would such a thing be for God? Why bother to labor so painstakingly with this present, deeply disappointing world? What is the point of that for an omnipotent deity? Again, we seem to be confronted with the portrait of a Creator whose character is such that there is a deep investment in the ongoing reality of the world of creation begun in Genesis 1—even if now that divine investment seems to be faltering and threatened.

We should appreciate, too, the extent to which this story describes an act of *de-creation*, or *un-creation*. On the second day, we recall, God had created a "dome" in the midst of the waters—those waters that had once swirled ominously as "a formless void," where "darkness covered the face of the deep" (1:6, 2). God's act of creation involved submitting all that whirling water to structure, to order, "separat[ing] the waters that were under the dome from the waters that were above the dome" (v. 7). But now, with this great deluge, "all the fountains of the great deep burst forth, and the windows of the heavens were opened" (7:11). God is allowing all those chaotic waters back in, imploding and inundating the structures that had made creaturely life possible. The point may be that just as humans already were tearing away the fabric of creation in their wickedness and violence, God responds in kind: the punishment fits the crime. If we are determined to undo God's good act of creation, if our rebellion undermines the structures of creation that make for life, then our Creator is willing to show us where our violence leads. Creation collapses. And yet . . .

Third, instead of destroying this world and creating a new one with a snap of the divine finger, *God saves this present world, and does so through a human being.* Perhaps all the world should be grateful that "Noah found favor in the sight of the LORD" (6:8)—but perhaps also we should suspect that if there had been no Noah to notice, God would have persisted in seeking a human partner. It is *adam,* humanity, after all, that has been created to serve as God's image, God's representative, within the realm of creation. As we will explore more extensively in chapter 5, John Wesley called this divine mandate for humanity the "political image": human beings are called to tend to the *polis,* the living community of all creatures (not only of humans) that dwell together on the earth. Certainly, Noah is called upon to fulfill precisely this task.

It should still fascinate us, though, that the Creator has such an interest in maintaining the order of this world, in sustaining its possibilities for life, even against the divine pronouncement of judgment: "I will blot out from the earth . . . people together with animals and creeping things and birds of the air, for I am sorry that I have made them" (v. 7). Further, we might wonder if it is worth all this trouble. Again, how difficult would it be for God simply to create a new batch of creatures—maybe an entirely new spate of species, including perhaps new and improved human beings—at the drop of a hat? This is painstaking work, finding a human who will cooperate with God's desire to save the world despite all this deep grief, sorrow, and wrath that God feels. And God calls Noah to build the ark—also a lot of work! We could further wonder why God does not just drop a ready-made ark from the heavens, or for that matter simply whisk up a representative bunch of creatures into heavenly safety, out of harm's way. But this ancient story renders God differently, and surprisingly. Instead of miracles of rescue, we encounter a human being doing some heavy lifting to build an ark of safety for himself, his family, and for earth's other living creatures. This biblical narrative, then, suggests once more that this world of creation in which we exist, along with all the other virtually countless species of creatures, is of deep importance to the Creator. Yet, surprisingly, the way in which God labors for the world's redemption is through the slow, risky, painstaking mode of collaboration with human creatures—and, more generally, with all of creation. This will emerge again as a critical theme in chapter 4 of this book, when we consider the Christian conviction that God's ultimate saving, or salving, of creation occurs through "the one man's [Jesus Christ's] obedience" (Rom. 5:19; see vv. 15, 17).

Fourth, it is only after the flood that we encounter in Scripture, for the first time, the language of *covenant*—and a very important covenant it is, for it is an *"everlasting covenant" with each and every creature* (Gen. 9:10, 15). This is a new beginning for creation. Indeed, just as in the beginning "a [*ruach*] from God swept over the face of the waters" (1:2), so now, after the flood, "God made a [*ruach*] blow over the earth, and the waters subsided" (8:1). Re-creation is underway for all the world's creatures—including human beings made in God's image—created to "image" or reflect God within the creaturely realm.

But will anything really be different? If human wickedness and violence presented such a disappointing problem to God before, why should anyone expect this second world—really, the same old world—to be any better? The biblical text clearly recognizes this quandary, and an intriguing reply is provided in divine speech. Before the flood "the LORD saw that the wickedness of humankind was great in the earth, and that every inclination of the thoughts of their hearts was only evil continually" (6:5)—hence the decision to purge the world. Compare this to the divine deliberations after the flood: "I will never again curse the ground because of humankind, for the inclination of the human heart is evil from youth; nor will I ever again destroy every living creature as I have done" (8:21). It is difficult to find much difference between these observations about humanity's deeply flawed character. God's reason for destroying the world becomes God's reason for pledging never again to destroy the world. What might this text be suggesting to us, its interpreters?

Our Covenantal God

Is it possible that God our Creator is narrated here as coming to terms with the stark limitations of creation, and especially of the creatures called *adam*? Does the text suggest that there was something in "the pleasing aroma" (8:21, NIV) of Noah's burnt offerings that aroused in the Creator some deeper understanding of the desires and drives within the human heart? Only now does God speak of "the fear and dread" of humans that "shall rest on every animal of the earth" (Gen. 9:2), for now "every moving thing that lives shall be food for you; . . . into your hand they are delivered" (vv. 3, 2). But even with this permission to hunt down animals for food, limitations are placed upon the human lust for animal flesh; eating it raw ("with its life, that is, its blood" [v. 4]) is prohibited, as is taking the life of a fellow human being ("for in his own image God made" *adam* or humanity [v. 6]).

The mention of raw flesh, blood, and murder together in the passage may signify that the Creator acknowledges that human beings can be driven hard by desires that, later, the rabbinic tradition would call *yetzer hara*—the "evil impulse." But perhaps "evil" is not quite the term. Jewish tradition meant by *yetzer hara* those attractions for what "gets our blood pumping," as we sometimes put it. Those desires, while in themselves natural and legitimate, can so easily become destructive; a healthy sense of friendly competition accelerates into cut-throat contests, the attraction for thrills and excitement degenerates into a thirst for blood, and sexual attraction and fascination readily transmute into lurid and predatory lust. In fallen humanity, these distortions of our desires seem virtually unavoidable. Hence, in God's judgment, "the inclination of the human heart is evil from youth" (8:21). Indeed, after the flood even Noah himself—God's new beginning for human beings!—is presented in distinctly unflattering ways (9:20-27).[3] Noah's story seems to serve as a grim commentary on the profound and lingering need of humanity to be renewed in the image of God. But such a renewal is not yet, at least as far as the stories of Genesis are able to take us.

Yet, thankfully, God "deals not with us according to our sins."[4] Instead, it is precisely in view of this deeper recognition of human rebellion that our Creator initiates a covenant. The narrative implies that God is adaptable, adopting the strategy of covenant as a mode of relation arising out of a stark assessment of the limitations of us frail and feeble creatures of flesh called *adam*—and, beyond us, of all of earth's creatures. In approaching us in terms of covenant rather than of perfectionistic expectations, God might be understood as coming to peaceful terms with our proneness to failure. It is remarkable how many times the covenantal promise is repeated: "As for me, I am establishing my covenant with you and your descendants after you, and with every living creature" (9:9-10); "I establish my covenant with you, that never again shall all flesh be cut off by the waters of a flood" (v. 11); "This is the sign of the covenant that I make between me and you and every living creature that is with you, for all future generations" (v. 12); the rainbow shall signify "the covenant between me and the earth" (v. 13), serving as a reminder of "my covenant that is between me and you and every living creature of all flesh" (v. 15); it shall be "the everlasting covenant between God and every living creature of all flesh that is on the earth" (v. 16); and then one last time: "This is the sign of the covenant that I have established between me and all flesh that is on the earth" (v. 17).

What is the promise of this everlasting covenant? That "never again shall all flesh be cut off by the waters of a flood, and never again shall there be a flood to destroy the earth" (v. 11). It is an everlasting covenant, a promise from the Creator to the creation to sustain its vitality and fruitfulness ("seedtime and harvest" [8:22]) as well as its predictability and reliability ("cold and heat, summer and winter, day and night" [v. 22]). It is an *everlasting covenant*, a promise given not simply to humans but to "every living creature of all flesh that is on the earth" (9:16).

The Fire Next Time?

It is a sad and all too predictable move in some Christian circles—even if it is also one with a long life in the history of the church's interpretation—to add quickly at this point, "The promise is never again to destroy the world with water; but it will be the fire next time!" Such a world-denying mentality is clearly at odds with this Genesis promise of an everlasting covenant. It is dismissive of Genesis's testimony regarding the Creator's intention for creation. It is very far from the spirit of this text to suppose that God holds a "fiery destruction" card up the divine sleeve. It is crucial in this regard to keep in mind that the flood is not simply "a flood"; rather, it is the removal of the protective structures of creation as described in Genesis 1 so that the primeval waters of "the deep" come rushing back in upon the dry land (cf. Gen. 1:9-10). If this is a sound interpretation, then the divine promise to refrain from flooding the world again is, more fundamentally, a promise to sustain its rhythms and processes indefinitely rather than to undo or destroy them.

Thus, the promise after the flood is not merely that God will not make it rain hard enough to flood us all away again—as though, instead, we should expect that a world-annihilating fire may descend any time now. Rather, and much more profoundly, the promise is for the maintenance of the order, predictability, reliability, goodness, and fruitfulness of the earth for the sake of all of its creatures—"birds and animals and every creeping thing that creeps on the earth—so that they may abound on the earth, and be fruitful and multiply on the earth" (8:17). In other words, it is a renewal of the promise of creation first pronounced in the blessings of Genesis 1, but this time the sense of divine blessing and promise is bound by an "everlasting covenant" made by God in full awareness of humanity's glaring weaknesses.

This is the first—and thus, arguably, the most cosmic, most comprehensive, most basic, most fundamental—covenant mentioned in Holy Writ. We may accordingly speculate as to its great importance for understanding how our Maker approaches creation, and with what intentions. We will surely attempt to understand its implications in the light of the coming of Jesus Christ, in whom, in Paul's words, "every one of God's promises is a 'Yes'" (2 Cor. 1:20)—that is, every promise receives divine ratification, divine reaffirmation, in Christ. This means that Jesus Christ fulfills and deepens the promises of God, including the covenantal promise of Genesis 9. Let us stress once more, then, particularly in the light of Christ, that Genesis 9 testifies to an "everlasting covenant *between God and every living creature of all flesh that is on the earth*" (v. 16). What if we really were to think of each and every one of earth's creatures as bound up in its own, particular covenantal relation with its Creator? And if we were to combine this notion with our earlier reflections about human beings as created to "image" or represent God toward all other creatures within the realm of creation? And if Christ is the very image of God, in whom all of God's covenantal promises receive their "Amen"? If all these things are true, what then is the human responsibility to "every living creature of all flesh that is on the earth" in the light of God's covenantal promise? It is likely that these are questions we have not yet sufficiently considered.

It may well be that the figure of Noah begins to provide an answer to such questions. In Noah, we recognize the critical role of human cooperation with God; the story demonstrates the necessity of human effort and planning, human sacrifice and self-denial, in order to labor with the Creator toward the goal of creation's well-being. What kinds of "arks" might need to be constructed today, in our time, for the sake of saving God's creation? How much effort is required? What is the hard work that we should be engaging in to labor with the Creator toward the goal of creation's well-being?

On the other hand, it might seem that if God has indeed promised to sustain the earth and its ecosystems indefinitely into the future, there is really nothing for us to worry about. Does God's promise guarantee a robust future for earth and its atmosphere? Perhaps, unlike Noah, we need not lift a finger for the sake of tending to the health of creation, because God will see to it with or without our cooperation. Since we live in the light of this first covenantal promise of God to sustain all of earth's generative processes, perhaps there is nothing for us to contribute.

What Has Happened to the Everlasting Covenant?

Given the fact that the everlasting covenant of Genesis 9 is, by all appearances, a unilateral promise from the Creator to sustain creation, it would indeed seem that all is well. What could possibly go wrong? We certainly do confess and believe that God is faithful to the divine promise (2 Cor. 1:18). And yet, as Old Testament scholar Ellen Davis has indicated in her insightful and challenging book *Scripture, Culture, and Agriculture*, Genesis 9 is not the last time that we see in Scripture the language of "the everlasting covenant," and what we see is not good.[5]

In the disorienting eschatological vision of Isaiah 24, creation itself is teetering on the brink: "Now the LORD is about to lay waste the earth and make it desolate, and he will twist its surface and scatter its inhabitants" (v. 1). Whatever it is, exactly, that the prophet envisions for the earth, no one is safe; social class and economic advantage will make no difference whatsoever (v. 2). The God who spoke the creative word "Let there be!" now speaks a destructive and despoiling word to the world in the prophetic utterance:

The earth dries up and withers,

the world languishes and withers;

the heavens languish together with the earth.

The earth lies polluted

under its inhabitants;

for they have transgressed laws,

violated the statutes,

broken the everlasting covenant.

Therefore a curse devours the earth,

and its inhabitants suffer for their guilt;

therefore the inhabitants of the earth dwindled,

and few people are left.

The wine dries up,

the vine languishes,

all the merry-hearted sigh.

. . . the gladness of the earth is banished.

(Vv. 4-7, 11)

Davis follows other biblical scholars in finding a critical connection between Genesis and Isaiah at the point of the language of "the everlasting covenant"—a covenant that Isaiah 24 proclaims human beings to have broken.[6] For example, Brevard Childs writes,

The earth has become polluted from the violation of God's laws and disregard of his statutes. Because of the mention of divine law, some commentators have proposed that the prophet is referring to the Mosaic covenant, yet this interpretation is very unlikely. The immediate reference to breaking the "everlasting covenant" offers a linguistic warrant for seeing rather a reference to the covenant with Noah (Gen 9:16). In addition, the scope of the account is not limited to Israel, but includes the entire world. The curse lies upon the whole world, and its inhabitants suffer the guilt.[7]

But how can it be that the entire world of human beings has "broken the everlasting covenant" if in fact God alone entered into that covenant unilaterally—apart from human participation, vows, or agreement? How is it that *human beings* break a covenant that *God alone* established: "I establish my covenant with you, that never again shall all flesh be cut off by the waters of a flood, . . . I will remember my covenant that is between me and you and every living creature of all flesh; and the waters shall never again become a flood to destroy all flesh" (Gen. 9:11, 15)? If this covenant is God's promise never to un-create creation, how and why are we humans implicated?

One daunting possibility is that while it is indeed God who initiated this everlasting covenant, the Creator to whom the Scriptures bear witness continues to create human beings in the divine image. As we have suggested, this is understood in the Bible primarily in functional terms, that is, human beings are called upon by God to "image" or reflect God, to represent God, within the realm of creation. God continues to create human beings to fulfill this responsibility. If this is so, then a sobering implication is that even while God makes unilateral promises to creation and indeed to every living creature, it is nonetheless God's desire and expectation, at least ideally, that we humans represent the Creator by enacting those promises in our everyday actions. Because we are the creatures who are graciously created in the image of God, God our Creator still is expecting us to fulfill the promise of divine faithfulness to creation.

There is good reason to wonder whether we are up to the task. Ironically, while we continue to debate the issue of global warming and whether or not, and to what extent, human technology, population, and activity have played a role—we may in fact be on the verge of another flood, of sorts. In the last forty-five years, the sea level has increased approximately two hundred millimeters (close to eight inches) on the world's coasts, flooding large areas of low-lying countries and small island nations.[8] In the award-winning short film titled *Sun Come Up* we learn about the plight of three thousand Carteret Pacific Islanders who had to relocate to another community off Papua New Guinea because the six islands on which they had long lived have recently been inundated by sea water. Erosion, the loss of their wells from saltwater incursion, destruction of their agricultural gardens, and other problems have made the Carteret people some of the world's first climate refugees.[9]

But the Carteret Islanders are just the beginning. It is expected that in the next fifty to one hundred years more than eighteen thousand people will become homeless in Tuamotus, a group of seventy-eight small islands in the Pacific about two hundred miles northeast of Tahiti.[10] According to United Nations estimates, as many as 250 million people worldwide could be affected by sea-level-rise flooding by the middle of this century and, if carbon emissions keep growing at the pace they are now, we will see more than a three-foot rise by the end of the present century.[11] Such a rise in sea level would cause flooding in several major coastal cities, among them Miami, Venice, New York City, and New Orleans, not to mention the loss of millions of acres of wetlands that are home to many endemic plants and animals.[12]

All of this is particularly sobering as we recall that the Genesis flood can be readily interpreted as an act of de-creation that is a just and appropriate judgment; as humanity inflicts destruction upon creation through sinful rebellion and violence, so God permits human beings to experience the logical outcome of their evil.[13] Are we now, in a sense, repeating this violence against God's good creation here on this planet? (Clearly, God's creation extends unimaginably, seemingly infinitely, beyond our beautiful little orb.) Virtually all climate scientists in the world agree that human activity is the cause for the increase in greenhouse gases (such as CO_2) over the past fifty years that are leading to a change in the climate on earth. In fact, when we look at natural events such as solar and volcanic activity, scientific models show that our planet would likely have cooled during the last fifty years instead of warmed. Instead, we see significant anthropogenic (*anthropo*, human; *genic*, generated or caused) warming because annual emissions of carbon dioxides (primarily from fossil fuels) increased by about 80 percent between 1970 and 2004.[14] Even formerly outspoken skeptics of human-induced global warming, the best known of whom is American physicist Richard Muller, have recently acknowledged that humans are responsible for the increase in carbon emissions that are leading to global climate change. It is a grim possibility that our material greed and addiction to comfort and convenience (particularly in the Northern hemisphere), our apathy and our refusal to face the data honestly, mean that we have yet again "broken the everlasting covenant" (Isa. 24:5) between the Creator and creation.

The Persistence of Our Covenantal God

Yet we have no reason to believe that God has given up on the project of creation, nor on human beings as the creatures called upon to "image" or reflect God within it. Indeed, our argument in the following chapter is that Jesus Christ—truly God, truly human—is the ultimate embodiment of divine faithfulness to the covenantal promises, including those made to "every living creature of all flesh" (Gen. 9:15). In fact, later in the prophecies of Isaiah we read that

God speaks comfort to a failed and forlorn Israel precisely by recalling that very first covenant:

This is like the days of Noah to me;

Just as I swore that the waters of Noah

would never again go over the earth,

so I have sworn that I will not be angry with you

and will not rebuke you.

For the mountains may depart

and the hills be removed,

but my steadfast love shall not depart from you,

and my covenant of peace shall not be removed,

says the LORD, who has compassion on you.

(Isa. 54:9-10)

In the next chapter of Isaiah, we encounter once more the language of "an everlasting covenant" (55:3)—this time in a hopeful way, perhaps even in direct answer to the earlier "doomsday" language of chapter 24. Can this language of "an everlasting covenant" still be legitimately connected, through interpretation, to the everlasting covenant of Genesis 9? If it can—and we believe it can—then it is clearly a renewal and reconfiguration of the Noah covenant, for it is now rooted in God's "steadfast, sure love for David" (Isa. 55:3). Indeed, the prophet's imagery is rich in metaphors of nature that encourage readers to make precisely that reconnection with God's covenantal promises after the flood. There are "the rain and the snow [that] come down from heaven" to water the earth, sprouting "seed to the sower and bread to the eater" (v. 10); there are "mountains and . . . hills" that "burst into song" and trees that joyfully "clap their hands" (v. 12). Earth's restored fruitfulness, Isaiah prophesies, "shall be to the LORD for a memorial, for an *everlasting sign* that shall not be cut off" (v. 13). The possibilities of understanding the vision of Isaiah 55 as a renewing of the everlasting covenant—even when that covenant has been frighteningly and dangerously threatened in Isaiah 24—appear strong.

But is this all finally wishful thinking? Can we sustain such a hope for creation? What would it take to make Isaiah 55 a reality? We might be tempted to retreat to the apocalyptic vision of Isaiah 24—earth teetering on destruction, the everlasting covenant shattered—and suppose that creation's only hope lies in a dramatic, unilateral act of God. But why are we so often tempted to assume that God's purpose for human beings within creation, as narrated in Genesis 1, has been (or soon shall be) terminated? Is such a wish itself actually a denial of God's vocation for us, and thus, in fact, yet another indication of our fall into the power of sin? Are we shrinking from the calling God entrusts to us?

Let us keep in mind that the renewal of the language of "everlasting covenant," for Isaiah, is to be rooted now in God's "steadfast, sure love for David" (55:3). We Christians cannot help but read of God's "sure love for David" in the light of the coming of "Jesus the Messiah, the son of David" (Matt. 1:1). Christ is ultimately the validation of God's promise of redemption through the line of David (Matt. 21:9; 22:41-45)—including God's promise in Isaiah 55 to renew "an everlasting covenant" that extends to all creatures, including water and plants, mountains and trees, the earth itself. If this book is an exploration of what it means to be renewed in the image of God, living holy lives in God's good creation, we must now attempt to understand the nature of God's renewing labor in and through Jesus Christ, the "son of David" who is also "the last Adam" (1 Cor. 15:45). To this undertaking we now turn.

PART II
God, Our Re-Creator

4
RECAPITULATION AND RENEWAL

As surely as God is faithful, . . . the Son of God, Jesus Christ,
. . . was not "Yes and No";
but in him it is always "Yes." For in him
every one of God's promises is a "Yes."
—2 Cor. 1:18-20

Jesus, if still Thou art today as yesterday the same,
Present to heal, in me display the virtue of Thy name.
—Charles Wesley

IN THIS LETTER addressed long ago to the troubled Corinthian church, Paul assured his audience that his ministry was grounded in the faithfulness of God. This divine faithfulness, proclaimed the apostle, has been validated decisively, and eternally, through Jesus Christ. "In him every one of God's promises is a 'Yes.'" We do not assume that Paul necessarily had in mind the post-flood covenant described in Genesis 9 when he wrote these words; nonetheless, there is certainly no reason to exclude its promises of "an everlasting covenant," as explored in the previous chapter of this book, from consideration. Our argument is that in and through Jesus the Messiah—God's great and ultimate word of "Yes"!—we have received profound reassurance of God's covenantal promise to sustain creation even in the face of the prophetic judgment that we human beings have broken that covenant. It would appear that God has not quit on us. As Paul writes elsewhere, "The gifts and the calling of God are irrevocable" (Rom. 11:29). If that is the case, then we should assume that the divine calling of Genesis 1—that we human beings are to image God to all creation—truly continues even today to be viable and valid.

Indeed, in this chapter we will argue that the coming of Jesus Christ is divinely intended to restore and renew us in that calling to exist "in the image of God." We shall attempt to explore how, and why, this is the case by engaging the pertinent teachings of a handful of important Christian theologians of the early generations of the church. We suggest that a consistent theme begins to emerge from such an engagement: *salvation through Jesus Christ is a renewal of humanity, an ongoing process of healing all aspects of human existence.* For Christian faith, Christology (the doctrine of who Christ is) is thoroughly inseparable from soteriology (the doctrine of how Christ heals us). We find this motif emerging repeatedly in the church's early struggles to determine how most faithfully to confess that Jesus is the Christ, God's unique Savior for all of creation.

The Contribution of Irenaeus: Affirming the Goodness of the Body

The earliest Christian theologian to have dedicated sustained interest in the particular vocation for which we humans are created, and to which we are called, was Irenaeus, bishop of Lyons (in present-day France) in the mid to late second century. A careful reader of Scripture, Irenaeus noted that Genesis 1:26 uses a dual phrase—"in our *image*, according to our *likeness*"—and assumed this dual terminology must carry some theological significance. For Irenaeus, the phrase "in our image" refers to the capacities of reason and free will, which, according to Irenaeus, distinguish us humans from God's other living creatures.[1] Perhaps today we would expand his list to include such physiological characteristics as brain/body size ratio, the ability to walk erect, opposable thumbs, and so on; from there we might go on to add creativity, imagination, writing, ability to contemplate future possibilities, moral agency, and a sense of responsibility. No doubt the list of characteristics could be expanded; the point is that such capacities as Irenaeus associated with the image of God would be those natural to, and at least relatively unique to, the human species.

But it is important to understand that Irenaeus distinguished all this from the second phrase of Genesis 1:26, "according to our likeness." For him, our *likeness* to God has to do with our growing or maturing spiritually such that our characters actually come to resemble God through the empowerment of the Holy Spirit.[2] The *image* of God is given, we might say, in the very creation of human beings. The *likeness* of God—or better, the likeness *to* God—is a project, a calling, a work in the making. If we lacked the capacities that mark us as the *image* of God, then we would have no possibility of fulfilling the divine call to live in God's *likeness*. But of course being created in the image of God does not guarantee that we will actually achieve the calling of living like God. That all depends upon the ways in which we actually exercise those capacities for thought, creativity, imagination, choice, responsibility. Hence, Irenaeus insisted on a strong theological distinction between Genesis 1's phrases "in our image" and "according to our likeness."

Most biblical scholars today probably would not share Irenaeus's assumption that "image" and "likeness" in Genesis 1 were actually intended to imply this sort of dual significance. Instead, they tend strongly, and almost unanimously, to interpret this as a parallelism, a typically Hebraic way of emphasizing a single idea by saying it in two different ways.[3] If such scholarship is correct—and we assume that it is—then Irenaeus's distinction between "image" and "likeness" is not, strictly speaking, a teaching of Genesis 1.

However, this need not imply that Irenaeus's distinction is unhelpful or misleading; quite the opposite is the case. Irenaeus, and the theological tradition that grew out of his influence, did identify an important distinction. It is the distinction between our natural capacities and the uses to which we put them. History shows clearly that we human beings have exercised our physical, cognitive, and creative capacities in ways that have profoundly affected the natural environment, both for good and for ill, and of course we continue to do so. Further, we are becoming increasingly aware of those effects, increasingly sensitive to the impact that our presence and our actions make upon God's good earth and skies—particularly since the Industrial Revolution and the subsequent exponential growth in both our technological capacities and our population. The human power to exercise such extensive influence upon our environment, we might say, is due to our being created in God's *image*—as is the use of our intelligence to comprehend and communicate this simple but important concept. Meanwhile, how we choose to respond, individually and collectively, to our growing awareness of the role we play in our planet's future viability falls under the category of our being beckoned toward God's *likeness*.

Of course, both Scripture and experience quickly remind us that we human beings, *adam* as a collective whole, have fared poorly in our calling. We have not been a faithful likeness of God our Creator; all have sinned and fall short of the glory, or the likeness, of God. But there is nothing in Holy Writ to suggest that God's calling upon humanity has been canceled or forfeited. Genesis 1 still describes our human vocation. We have already noted in chapter 1 of this book that Psalm 8 reinforces this truth of God's calling upon human beings, who are "crowned [by God!] with glory and honor" (v. 5), to function as God's image in the world. In addition, we might note the glaring and unavoidable fact that, two millennia after the Messiah's coming, we human beings have not been delivered from our weighty responsibilities; indeed, we are increasingly faced with decisions that profoundly (and perhaps, in at least some instances, irreparably) impact the planet upon which we live, and upon which all living creatures of earth depend for their very lives.

What difference, then, has the coming of Jesus the Messiah made? Is the redemption he brings simply a rescue of souls out of this material world that is doomed for demise? Or ought we instead to think of salvation as a divine labor that is far more expansive, inclusive, and cosmic than what we might often imagine? Irenaeus certainly affirmed the second option. For him, Jesus is the Second Adam, whose faithful obedience to God has begun to turn the very stream of all creation back toward its good and loving Creator. This idea, often called the doctrine of recapitulation, lies at the heart of Irenaeus's profoundly biblical, and perennially pertinent, theology.

We can readily utilize Psalm 8 to help clarify Irenaeus's central conviction. Interestingly, and importantly, the New Testament quotes this psalm on two occasions. In both instances, what the psalmist sings about *adam*—that is, about all human beings—the New Testament applies to Jesus. In 1 Corinthians 15 Paul writes that "God has put all things in subjection under his feet" (v. 27). Whereas Psalm 8 means the "feet" or authority of humanity, it is immediately clear that Paul means the "feet" of Christ the Son. It should not surprise us that later in that same chapter Paul calls Jesus "the last Adam" (1 Cor. 15:45) and "the second man" (v. 47). Jesus the Son in some fashion sums up in himself, or recapitulates, all of humanity and the human vocation to image God. In fact, Paul in the same passage asserts that "just as we have borne the image of the man of dust, we will also bear the image of the man of heaven" (v. 49). The Second Adam restores and fulfills the first.

In the other New Testament citation, Hebrews, the passage sampled from Psalm 8 is even longer. "But someone has testified somewhere, 'What are human beings that you are mindful of them, or mortals, that you care for them? You have made them for a little while lower than the angels [Hebrews is quoting the Septuagint, the Greek translation of the Hebrew text, so some of the wording differs a little]; you have crowned them with glory and honor, subjecting all things under their feet'" (Heb. 2:6-8a). The passage then observes that in fact "we do not yet see everything in subjection to them, but we do see Jesus" (2:8b-9a), thereby implying that in some significant way God's vocation for humans—to function as the divine image within creation—has been decisively exemplified, or embodied, by Jesus. Indeed, the opening of Hebrews identifies the Son as "the reflection of God's glory" (1:3), which is the essential meaning of being the image and likeness of God. Where humanity, the collective *adam*, has failed in this high and holy calling, Jesus has faithfully and obediently succeeded.

It is important to emphasize, though, what Hebrews is claiming about Jesus's success in this regard. He is "now crowned with glory and honor [remember, this is language derived from Psalm 8] because of the suffering of death, so that by the grace of God he might taste death for everyone" (Heb. 2:9). What a remarkable and even shocking fulfillment of what it means to be the divine image! Jesus does not image God with overpowering majesty or overwhelming might but by "the suffering of death," by tasting death for everyone. Hebrews proceeds to proclaim that Christ fulfills the role of imaging God—the role described in Genesis 1 and reiterated in Psalm 8— through sharing in flesh and blood, participating fully in the human condition and the human calling, being "a merciful and faithful high priest in the service of God" and making "a sacrifice of atonement for the sins of the people" (Heb. 2:17).

Thus Christians cannot adequately reflect upon the idea of humanity in the image of God without immediately and first thinking of Jesus. And we cannot think of Jesus without thinking about his deep participation in human existence, including his redemptive suffering. Jesus Christ is "truly human," the last Adam, the True Human—and thus is also, and equally, "the image of the invisible God" (Col. 1:15). Precisely as "the image of the invisible God," we read in Colossians, "through him God was pleased to reconcile to himself all things, whether on earth or in heaven, by making peace through the blood of his cross" (v. 20). Jesus fulfills the calling of the True Human by offering himself fully for the sake of creation's redemption, embodying God's reconciliation to *"all things,* whether on earth or in heaven," and thus not only to human beings.

We insist again, however, that the ministry, death, and resurrection of Jesus should not be understood as negating or canceling our human vocation as described in Genesis 1 and echoed in Psalm 8. Jesus does not replace us or relieve us of our responsibility; rather, he represents us, faithfully *re-presenting* what it means to be a human being whose obedient life images God. Jesus does not cancel our calling as humans to live as God's image in creation; rather, he reveals to us what living "according to God's likeness" is intended by God to look like.

As God's Second Adam, the True Human, Jesus also is the root source of our healing and renewal, our transformation toward the true image of God (2 Cor. 3:18). Thus, Colossians later instructs us to abandon lives of anger, malice, wrath, abuse, and falsehood, making it evident that Jesus's faithful obedience does not cancel out our own. Rather, we are called by God to actual, day-to-day holiness, "seeing that [we] have stripped off the old self [the 'old Adam,' we used to call it] with its practices and have clothed [our]selves with the new self, which is being renewed in knowledge according to the image of its creator" (3:9-10). *Being renewed in knowledge according to the image of its creator*—and Christ is that veritable image of the invisible God, the Creator. Jesus Christ's very words and works provide us the knowledge of who God is and what God is like—a knowledge in which we may be renewed and in which we are called to live by the power of the Spirit of Christ (Rom. 8:9-11).

Let us be careful to stress, then, that stripping off the old self includes being rid of its destructive practices; the passage specifically mentions "anger, wrath, malice, slander, and abusive language" (Col.

3:8). Similarly, it describes the practices of the new self as "compassion, kindness, humility, meekness, and patience[,] bear[ing] with one another . . . forgiv[ing] each other" and, "above all, . . . love, which binds everything together in perfect harmony" (vv. 12-14). The basic point is that our renewal in God's image through Christ is not abstract, theoretical, or ethereal; it is certainly not just a ticket to heaven when we die. Rather, our Creator intends renewal in Christ to be actual, practical, embodied in everyday existence in the world. Thus, Christ's renewal of our human nature and existence does not leave us "off the hook" to do as we please. Presumably, this important truth would equally apply to the calling upon human lives as we have discovered it in our interpretation of Genesis 1:26-31. It would not suffice simply to proclaim that Christ has fulfilled the role of imaging God, such that we no longer need be bothered with our responsibilities for creation's well-being as entrusted to us by the Creator.

Irenaeus developed a particularly compelling description of this renewal of humanity through Jesus Christ. Drawing primarily upon the Adam/Christ argument in Romans 5:12-21—that, in essence, "the one man's obedience" has overcome "the one man's disobedience" (v. 19)—Irenaeus perceived the critical importance of insisting upon Jesus's true humanity. If Jesus were not a true, real, and physical human being, then whatever else he might be, he would not be truly connecting with us; in that case, his obedience would provide no true reply to our disobedience. Such a Christ as that would not be uniting with human creatures in a creaturely and finite world. But it is only such a union, Irenaeus insisted, that provides us, and all of creation, the path of healing. In his classic text *Against Heresies*, Irenaeus wrote that all the heretics he was opposing shared certain ideas in common: "They allege that the Word, the Christ, never came into this world, and that the Savior was neither incarnate nor suffered." Consequently, "according to none of the views of the heretics was the Word of God made flesh."[4]

This is a crucial point. Irenaeus was not arguing for the true incarnation of the Word simply on the basis of proof texts from the Bible. Irenaeus was instead building a biblical argument about *how salvation actually occurs*. It happens, essentially, through a true recapitulation of human existence, of human nature and obedience, as originally intended by our Creator. Irenaeus understood the incarnation itself, then, to be of saving, or healing ("salving"), significance. "Vain are those who say that his appearance [i.e., Christ's appearance as a human being] was a mere fiction. . . . [For] to say that his appearance was only seeming is the same as to say that he took nothing from Mary."[5] If it were really the case that Jesus "took nothing from Mary," then he would not have truly shared in our humanity. It would mean that the Word received nothing from the creaturely realm in the act of entering the world. Though this was precisely what at least some gnostic Christian groups wanted to think about Jesus, Irenaeus vehemently resisted. If the gnostics were right about Jesus, then "he would not have had real flesh and blood"; if that were the case, then he could not have "recapitulated in himself the ancient making of Adam."[6] For Irenaeus and many who would follow in his influence, it is precisely in this recapitulation of "the ancient making of Adam" that we are offered restoration and renewal.

How does this recapitulation touch and transform our lives? Is it merely a teaching that we perhaps decide to accept as true? What difference does this teaching make? How does Jesus's renewal and fulfillment of "the ancient making of Adam" reach into our present existence? These are crucial questions at the heart of this book. Let us begin to answer them by noting that, for Irenaeus and the rest of second-century Christianity, our participation in the Lord's Table is one of the fundamental practices by which God in Christ offers us restoration and healing. Hence, in one of the most moving passages of Christian theological writing ever, Irenaeus interweaved the themes of God's creation, the Word's incarnation, and our participation in the Lord's Supper into a tapestry of salvation. This sacrament involves actual bread that we eat and the cup that we drink; we physically ingest these gifts of the earth into our material bodies. Irenaeus argued that if God does not love and intend to save our bodies,

> then neither did the Lord redeem us by his blood, nor is the cup of the Eucharist the communion of his blood, and the bread which we break the communion of his body. For blood is only to be found in veins and flesh, and the rest of human nature, which the Word of God was indeed made [partaker of, and so] he redeemed us by his blood. . . . For since we are his members, and are nourished by creation—and he himself gives us this creation, making the sun to rise, and sending the rain as he wills—he declares that the cup, from the creation, is his own blood, by which he strengthens our blood, and he has firmly assured us that the bread, from the creation, is his own body, from which our bodies grow. . . . [Given this,] how can they say that [the body] cannot receive the free gift of God, which is eternal life, since it is nourished by the body and blood of our Lord, and made a member of him?[7]

There is the real flesh-and-blood body of Jesus, who broke bread and said to his disciples, "This is my body, . . . broken for you" (1 Cor. 11:24, KJV). There is the wheat that grew from the soil and was ground into flour to make that bread. There are the grapes that emerged from the vines whose roots probed the earth for moisture and nutrients. There is the sun's energy-rich light, and living organisms' release of carbon dioxide, that contributed significantly to the growing of those stalks of wheat and clusters of grapes. And here are our human bodies—skin, bone, blood, organs—that require daily nourishment, "our daily bread." Somehow, Irenaeus observed, all of these precious realities are intertwined in the redemptive, renewing, recapitulating labor of God our Creator through Jesus the Incarnate Son.

Accordingly, salvation is profoundly grounded in this world of flesh and bone, of soil and water, of sunlight and air. Even as we are created in God's image to grow increasingly in God's likeness, Irenaeus argued, we do this as bodily creatures in a material world.

We do not leave our bodies or material reality behind. Ignatius of Antioch, another second-century Christian leader, similarly warned his readers about gnostic Christians who denied the reality of Jesus's material body and his physical suffering. These people, wrote Ignatius, shied away from celebration of the Lord's Supper because its words of institution are so thoroughly *bodily*: "This is my body; . . . this is my blood." And on a related note, Ignatius immediately added, "They have no care for love—none for the widow, none for the orphan, none for the afflicted, none for the prisoner, none for the hungry or thirsty."[8] Ignatius's observation implies a deep connection between how we think about Jesus and how we live our everyday lives. If our Christianity is fixated only on "spiritual realities," then widows and orphans or prisoners or the hungry and thirsty will likely lie beneath our superspiritual interests. Such a view of Christianity is the practical denial of the incarnation.

Given Ignatius's and Irenaeus's robust emphasis upon Jesus's truly material existence as a body, we are pushed to think hard about how our bodily existence impacts, influences, and interacts with the rest of the physical world. The doctrine of the incarnation of the Word underscores the truth that our lives as bodies—radically dependent as we are upon nourishment, rest, and protection from the elements—are deeply intertwined with all of the rest of God's creatures who have the same basic needs. Bodies matter to God; indeed, all matter matters. This, of course, includes each and every one of our bodies. The direct implication is that the Christian doctrine of salvation, rooted deeply in the incarnation of the Word, impels us to take godly care of our bodies. Christian discipleship includes the responsibility to seek healthy nourishment, preventive healthcare, and adequate rest and shelter—and that we work toward the fulfillment of these basic bodily goods for all people.

The incarnation hallows all of human life and all human lives; in fact, the incarnation hallows all of creation. If this is so, then surely it matters how we live together with one another, and with all other living creatures, as material bodies in a material world. As those creatures called upon to reflect the character of the Creator, we human beings are uniquely gifted to reflect on these issues and live accordingly in divine Wisdom. That very Wisdom became flesh and lived among us creatures of flesh: this bears deep ramifications for the manner of our living among all of God's creatures—that is, to draw from the language of Genesis 9, among *all flesh*.

The Contribution of Gregory of Nazianzus: Affirming the Goodness of the Mind

If God's Word truly did become flesh and dwelt among us as the first-century Jew Jesus of Nazareth, how has this momentous act of God affected our renewal in the divine image? What differences should a divine labor like this make in the way we actually live our daily lives? These are the kinds of questions we are pursuing in this chapter, with the help of a trio of Christian thinkers from the church's early generations.

A couple of centuries after the time of Irenaeus, a new controversy arose regarding the human nature of Jesus. A teacher named Apollinaris from Alexandria, Egypt, tried to resolve the mystery of the union of the divine and human natures by suggesting that while Jesus had a human body, his "rational soul" or mind was not human at all. Rather, the preexistent Logos described in John 1:1-13, opined Apollinaris, had descended into a human body and essentially "replaced" what would have been the human mind of the person named Jesus of Nazareth. "So Christ," he wrote, "having God as his spirit—his intellect ['rational soul' or mind]—together with [animal] soul and body, is rightly called 'the human being from heaven.' He is not a human being but is like a human being, since he is not coessential with humanity in his highest part [i.e., in the mind or mental life]."[9]

For Apollinaris, then, the Logos or divine intellect simply found—or more precisely, created—a body to inhabit and control. This is comparable to a puppeteer pulling strings or, even closer, a ventriloquist moving the dummy's "body" and mouthing its words. Apollinaris believed that the human mind was far too weak—prone to distraction, temptation, and forgetfulness—to have been a dimension of Jesus's earthly experience.

It should be obvious that, whatever sort of being Apollinaris might have believed he was describing, it is not a truly human being; indeed, he said as much. Thus the being that Apollinaris imagined Jesus to be is not one that actually participates in the deeply textured layers of our existence—for we are not only physical beings but also mental, spiritual, emotional, volitional, and so on. Further, these various dimensions of our existence are inextricably interweaved with one another. One of the gospel descriptions of Jesus that most clearly reflects this very idea is that, throughout his youth, "Jesus increased in wisdom and in years, and in divine and human favor" (Luke 2:52). Apollinaris's Christology was hard-pressed to make any real sense of this intriguing statement; if Jesus "increased in wisdom," growing intellectually as well as physically, spiritually, and socially ("in divine and human favor"), then his mind must have shared in the creaturely limitations of all other human minds. Jesus is not the Logos masquerading behind a human face and body.

Apollinaris had served as a kind of theological apprentice to Athanasius, the great champion of the orthodox confession about Christ's dual natures as described at the Council of Nicea (325). So Apollinaris undoubtedly possessed a measure of credibility, perhaps even respectability, among the churches of northern Africa. Further, it is not entirely obvious that he believed anything so terribly different from his celebrated mentor. He did, however, state more explicitly some ideas about Jesus Christ that had been left relatively undefined by Athanasius. It is obvious that Apollinaris insisted upon a strong recognition of Jesus's real and true material body; at least on this issue, Irenaeus would have been pleased. However, there is every reason to suspect that Irenaeus would have roundly rejected Apollinaris's notion that Jesus's human body simply housed a divine mind. For this surely would *not* have been a recapitulating of "the ancient making of Adam," to revisit Irenaeus's lovely phrase—for "the ancient making of Adam" implies a truly human being with human faculties. If this is so, then Jesus must have had an authentic human brain that developed in the particular ways of a first-century Jewish male of Galilee.

It is no surprise, then, that one of the fourth-century theologians most influenced by the Irenaean tradition—indeed a significant contributor to that tradition—provided a remarkably forceful rejection of Apollinaris's Christology. Gregory of Nazianzus (330-390) peered deeply into the problem created by Apollinaris's thinking and wrote, in scathing reply, what has become one of the most famous passages in Christian theology:

> If anyone has put his trust in him as a man without a human mind, he is really bereft of mind, and quite unworthy of salvation. For that which the Logos has not assumed he has not healed; but that which is united to his Godhead is also saved. If only half of Adam fell, then that which Christ assumes and saves may be half also; but if the whole of his nature fell, it must be united to the whole nature of the One that was begotten, and so be saved as a whole.
>
> Let them not, then, begrudge us our complete salvation, or clothe the Savior only with bones and nerves and the portraiture of humanity. . . . [For] if he has a soul [i.e., true bodily life], and yet is without a mind, how is he man?—for man is not a mindless animal. . . . But if his humanity is intellectual and not lacking mind, let them cease to be thus really mindless.[10]

Gregory realized that the Apollinarian position was essentially that "the Godhead took the place of the human intellect." He immediately asks the fundamental question: "How does this touch me?"[11] Gregory understood that Jesus Christ does not deliver us from our true humanity, but truly participates in our humanity to redeem and restore it. "Keep then the whole human being," Gregory insisted—and *we* must now, in our time, also "keep then the whole human being." We must insist that the whole human being is a creature who is deeply interconnected not only with all other people but with all other living creatures, and indeed with all of creation. We must recognize, probably more deeply than Gregory did, that our true humanity is deeply rooted, profoundly enmeshed, in this material world whose well-being has been entrusted into our care.

Further, "the whole human being" does include, as Gregory insisted, a human mind. God has created the human mind and, through the incarnation of the Word, is healing and restoring the human mind. Minds matter to God! Human beings are intended by our Creator to be creatures who understand, and respond faithfully to, the divine calling to image God among all of the rest of God's creatures on earth. The human mind or intellect—what Gregory and others of his culture called "the rational soul"—is utterly necessary to this divine calling. We need to use our minds well as we strive to exercise godly, or Christlike, dominion within God's creation. Indeed, the question of how human beings ought now to live, in the wake of our patterns of behavior and consumption that have brought our planet to the brink, will require the finest of human reflection, creativity, and imagination in the decades to come. Thus, the task of imaging or reflecting God requires careful, responsible, rational reflection. No wonder that Gregory insisted that our human minds need renewing through Jesus Christ—and following the logic already laid out by Irenaeus two centuries earlier, he argued that our minds are not and cannot be renewed if Jesus himself did not have a real human mind.

Gregory acknowledged that Apollinaris's position relied heavily upon a particular interpretation of John 1:14, "And the Word became flesh and lived among us." It appears that Apollinaris interpreted "flesh" to mean nothing more than a body—and the body he had in mind was really little more than an outer shell inside of which the Word existed as the Divine Mind. The Logos, for him, had entered into a human body like a hand into a glove. It appears, unfortunately, that John 1:14 has far too often been interpreted in essentially this way. But this interpretation of the Greek word *sarx* ("flesh") is, we believe, wholly inadequate for bearing the meaning that John's gospel intends.

Perhaps the most effective way to get at the point we hope to make is to note the words that were not employed in John 1:14. We do not read that the Word became *Ioudaios*, a Jew, even though that is indeed the case, and even though this gospel later explicitly associates the salvation Jesus brings with the Jewish people (4:22). Nor does John 1:14 proclaim that the Word became *anēr* (male), though in fact that is the case, for Jesus was a first-century Jewish male. The text does not even state that the Word became *anthrōpos*, though indeed it is also true that Jesus was a human being. So why would the text read, instead, *o logos sarx egeneto*—"the Word became *flesh*"?

We believe it is highly illuminating to read this term *sarx* against the backdrop of the Hebrew Bible's usage of the term *basar*, translated in the Septuagint as *sarx*. Indeed, we have already encountered this word concept in an extremely crucial way in Genesis (9:15-17).[12] "Flesh" signifies creaturely existence, particularly understood to be finite, vulnerable, frail, mortal. It is the realm of creaturely existence in all of its limitations.[13] "All flesh is grass"—here today, gone tomorrow—that readily withers under the hot winds of divine breath (Isa. 40:6; Ps. 103:15). Another biblical metaphor for this idea of creaturely finitude is "dust": "If [God] should . . . gather to himself his breath, all flesh would perish together, and all mortals return to dust" (Job 34:14-15); but God, "being compassionate, . . . remembered that they were but flesh, a wind that passes and does not come again" (Ps. 78:38-39). King Hezekiah encouraged the people of Judah by reminding them that hordes of the invading Assyrian king were but "an arm of flesh" (2 Chron. 32:8)—nothing but fellow finite creatures.

It is important, then, to interpret "flesh" in a far broader fashion than simply as the material covering our bones. Of course, the stuff covering our bones is part of the realm of the flesh, but "flesh" cannot be limited simply to skin. *"Flesh" is the realm of living, creaturely existence.* So to read that "the Word became flesh," if this interpretation is correct, is to learn that the very Logos of God, who shares in the very being of God, has entered so thoroughly, participated so fully, in the realities of creaturely existence as to have *become* that creaturely reality.

To become "flesh," accordingly, places the Logos in full solidarity, a thorough sharing, with all creatures. This in turn implies that the incarnation's salving significance is not limited to human beings. The incarnation is the Creator's thorough and intimate union with, and sharing in, the full realm of living creatures. Of course, the Word became a human being, a male, yes, a Jewish male; the point is that the incarnation—this radical and dramatic *becoming flesh*—fully entails the Word's full immersion in the complex, living web of creaturely existence. All creatures are intertwined, and so the Word's incarnation as a first-century Jewish male entails the Word's full participation in *flesh*, the realm of creaturely finitude, frailty, vulnerability, pain, and death.

In terms of Gregory's opposition to Apollinaris, of course, the Word's true incarnation as a human being must include the vulnerability and frailty of the human mind. For otherwise our minds are not healed—and God, Gregory insisted, certainly intends to redeem our capacities for thought, imagination, and creativity. They are utterly necessary to our faithful obedience to God's calling that we function as the divine image within the realm of creation.

If this Word is indeed truly *God*, what does the incarnation accomplish for creation? What is it that we receive through Christ? In and through Jesus of Nazareth, the Word Incarnate, we receive the very presence of God, who is Love, in precious union with the creature. We are reunited with the very Power and Origin of creation.

God the Creator has become Immanuel, God with us. Love is our healing. So ran the argument of Maximus the Confessor.

The Contribution of Maximus the Confessor: Affirming the Goodness of Volition

A few centuries after the Apollinarian controversy, Christians were embroiled in yet another important question about Jesus. Did he have a human will? Did he experience the challenges of making hard decisions? Did circumstances force him to make meaningful moral choices in his life? Was he really tempted to sin, to choose against God's will? "The topic may appear arcane," writes Robert Louis Wilken, "yet in this debate Christian thinkers of the time, by attending closely to a single event in Christ's life, were able to express the nature of Christ's humanity more clearly than any had done earlier."[14] That single event was Jesus's passionate prayer in the garden of Gethsemane, and the most important of these thinkers who reflected on Gethsemane was Maximus the Confessor (580-662). His interpretation of Jesus's prayer adds another important layer to our understanding of the incarnation as the way in which God brings healing to creation.

During Maximus's lifetime, Greek-speaking Christians of the eastern rim of the Mediterranean Sea were again divided on the question of how to understand Jesus's humanity. Many, including the emperor, Constans II, believed that Jesus did not have a human will, and so could not have experienced the typical human struggle to discern, let alone to fulfill, God's will. For these Christians, the only "will" that operated in Jesus's consciousness was the will of God. Thus, we might say it today, doing the will of God was, for him, automatic and inevitable. This position became known as monothelitism (Gk., "one will").

Maximus was not alone in questioning this portrait of Christ's moral experience, but he was probably the most insistent. He appealed to Jesus's words, "Not my will but yours be done" (Luke

22:42*b*), and asked whether that prayer really made sense if Jesus did not actually have a will, a desire, in this matter. And surely he had just expressed his will by praying, "Father, if you are willing, remove this cup from me" (22:42*a*).[15] Jesus faces stark uncertainty and desires to explore possibilities other than betrayal, arrest, and crucifixion. Indeed, it is only within the context of such uncertainty and temptation that his commitment to accomplish his Father's will becomes morally meaningful. This is real obedience in the midst of harsh struggle, not someone gliding along on automatic pilot. In the words of Hebrews, "Although he was a Son, he *learned obedience through what he suffered*" (5:8).

Maximus put the matter this way: "If the Word made flesh does not himself will naturally as a human being and accomplish things in accordance with his human nature, how can he willingly undergo hunger and thirst, labor and weariness, sleep and everything else common to humanity?"[16] This is a lovely question, demonstrating that Maximus understood that to be truly human means to share fully in human nature and its limitations, as well as its fulfillments. We cannot have a Savior who is a cut-and-paste human being; if "the Word became flesh and lived among us," then full immersion in the life of the flesh (creaturely reality), in all of its deep interconnections, is necessary and inevitable. Maximus's holistic vision of human existence connects deeply with contemporary sensibilities. It also reminds us that our human will or volition, redeemed through Christ's own faithful obedience, is a critical and necessary aspect of our renewal in the divine image.

It might be interjected at this very point that if Jesus were truly human, he would have to have sinned. But the implication in that idea is that sin is a necessary element or aspect of human nature. It is not. It is *fallen* human beings who are sinful and who commit sin; indeed, sin is a perversion and a compromise, rather than an inherent aspect, of human nature. We might put it this way: sin makes us less than human, not fully or truly human. It drags us downward, away from our true identity and calling. We are created to image God, who is holy love. Humanity's collective falling short of this holy calling, becoming instead embroiled in destructive and addictive patterns of idolatry, is a fundamental definition of sin. On the other hand, Jesus, the true and final *adam*, "has been tempted as we are, yet without sin" (Heb. 4:15, ESV).

We should appreciate how Maximus's argument sustains the tradition of thought developed by Irenaeus in his reading of Romans 5. "For just as by the one man's disobedience the many were made sinners, so by the one man's obedience the many will be made righteous" (v. 19). The obedience of "the one man," Jesus, must be every bit as real, every bit as human in terms of actual volition, as humanity's collective disobedience has been. This is essentially the extension of the church's earlier affirmations that Jesus had (or was!) a real human body and a real human mind; so, also, Jesus faced and made real human decisions. This led Maximus to the conviction that precisely in his hard-fought obedience to God's will as a human, Jesus "willed and carried out our salvation."[17] Indeed, in his obedience as "the last Adam" (1 Cor. 15:45) Jesus reveals that "the human will is not less human but more human because it is in harmony with the divine will."[18] Even so, for harmony to be *real harmony*, more than one voice—or, in this matter before us, more than one will—is required. Extending this musical metaphor, we might say that God desires harmony. To put it more biblically, it is God's desire to labor covenantally with creation, as we have suggested especially in chapter 3—and now Jesus's full and true humanity underscores and validates this crucial biblical vision of our Creator. In Jesus we encounter the decisive revelation, the ultimate unveiling of God precisely *in* (2 Cor. 5:19) and *with* (Acts 10:38) a human who is a truly human being—body, mind, will, and whatever else would be considered necessary to a truly human existence. The incarnation of the Word upon which Irenaeus, Gregory, and Maximus heartily insisted demonstrates that God is pleased to co-labor with us and, indeed, with all creation—"all flesh."

We call Maximus "the Confessor" precisely because he worked out these ideas in the face of growing political opposition; not only the emperor but also the patriarch of Constantinople embraced monothelitism. Sadly, Christians thought that differences over this question could be settled by inflicting pain on their fellow believers. Maximus was first imprisoned and then exiled for refusing to submit to the emperor's theological dictates; later, he was brought back from exile to see if he had changed his mind. He had not. At the conclusion of this second trial, his right hand was cut off so that he would no longer write about Jesus as he had, and his tongue was ripped out so that he would no longer speak of a Jesus who possessed a truly human will. He died shortly thereafter, earning the nickname "the Confessor." What he "confessed" against all opposition was a whole Christ: not a Christ-spirit who lived above and beyond the needs and limitations of a material body; not a Christ-mind who occupied an otherwise mindless, soulless physical body; and not a Christ-robot who automatically and effortlessly carried out the divine will because he knew nothing of temptation, self-determination, or meaningful choice. He confessed that the divine Word had become *flesh* in all of its entailments.

We recall the earlier insight of Gregory of Nazianzus—"that which the Logos has not assumed he has not healed; but that which is united to his Godhead is also saved"—for with Maximus, we come to appreciate that human agency is both created and redeemed by God. This means that our everyday lives, and what we decide to do as bodies together in a material world, are of saving significance to our Maker. We have choices to make that will impact the world around us for generations to come. The choices that we make, and the reasons we make them, really do count. God has validated this in Jesus Christ, the Second Adam. God has created us with true agency and responsibility, and through the incarnation of the

Word it becomes clear that God has no intention of removing these weighty but wonderful gifts from us. God the Creator does indeed desire to redeem creation, but not apart from us human creatures to whom God has given moral responsibility as the creatures called to reflect God in the world. Our God is a covenantal God. Jesus Christ is the perfect portrait of that covenantal relationship, the ideal embodiment of God and human being working together.

There is considerable irony in the fact that Maximus lost his tongue and his writing hand—critical components of his own human experience as a communicative being—because he insisted upon the fully human nature and experience of Jesus the Lord, the Word Incarnate. The point of his argument was that God creates us, and desires to save or salve us, as whole creatures. His vision of salvation was profoundly holistic, for he understood the whole human to be relational and deeply intertwined within the much larger environment of all creation: "For humanity clearly has the power of naturally uniting [all things in creation, and so] . . . can come to be the way of fulfillment of what is divided . . . lifting up [all things] to God and fully accomplishing union."[19] For Maximus, human beings in relation with one another are called upon by God to be agents of reconciliation throughout creation. Maximus derived this idea from Genesis 1 and the teaching that human beings, male and female, are created in the divine image. For Maximus, this implied primarily the human role of laboring toward peace and harmony throughout all aspects of God's creation.

Even if we suspect that Maximus may have valued the human contribution too highly, his vision is clearly a pertinent one for us today. He raises the question of how we human beings—and Christians in particular—ought to live in this world such that reconciliation among all creatures is approximated if not realized. How ought we to live, in the light of this eschatological goal? Maximus perceived that there are many layers of creation in and through which human beings, as potential agents of divine reconciliation, are called upon to labor. "And finally," he rhapsodized, "the human person unites the created nature with the uncreated [i.e., God] through love—O, the wonder of God's love for us human beings!—showing them to be united and one through the possession of grace, the whole [creation] entirely interpenetrated by God"![20]

This is a remarkable vision of the human role, as entrusted to us by our Creator, for laboring toward creation's healing and well-being. Maximus dreamed of human beings living in God's creation in such a way that it would be "entirely interpenetrated by God," shot through and through with divine love. This would seem, ultimately, to be possible only by a decisive act of God, popularly associated with the end of the world. Maximus, however, is not envisioning the end of the world but rather is stipulating that the world's true "end" or purpose is to be indwelt by human creatures who image God by living and acting in love toward all things.

Of course, we have failed in this high and holy calling. We are fallen sinners, and sin harms ourselves, other people, and God's good, green earth. Creation, at least here on planet Earth, is not thriving in the love of God. "We know that the whole creation has been groaning in labor pains until now," Paul writes (Rom. 8:22). But God, Maximus insisted, has begun the quiet labor of redemption, of healing, of reconciliation through the fully human, fully divine life of Jesus. This Word Incarnate "fulfills the great purpose of God the Father, 'to recapitulate everything both in heaven and earth in himself' (Eph. 1:10), 'in whom everything has been created' (Col. 1:16)," Maximus wrote. "Thus he divinely recapitulates the universe in himself, showing that the whole creation exists as one, . . . completed by the gathering together of its parts one with another in itself."[21]

Hopefully, we may begin to appreciate how Maximus's full-bodied Christology is thoroughly consonant with his visionary ideas about salvation as God's work of universal reconciliation brought about through human agency. Jesus must have exercised truly human volition within the conditions of "flesh" as we have defined this word concept, for if he did not, then he has not recapitulated in himself the reality of human nature—nor the fundamental human calling to reflect God's matchless love to every person, indeed to every creature, throughout creation.

Finally, what the christological battles of Irenaeus, Gregory, and Maximus teach us is that Christian faith understands creation, and salvation, *incarnationally*. God does not save us by divine fiat, by pronouncement from on high. This is not magic. Rather, God salves us, heals us and indeed all of creation—all "flesh"—through a thorough participation in creaturely reality, "from within." God's ultimate revelation to all of earth's creatures has been in and through this particular human being, Jesus the Christ. Of course, creaturely reality is not exhausted by human nature—far from it!—but it includes human nature: body, mind, volition. God, through the incarnation of the Word, has "assumed" or taken on, has truly and fully "shouldered," all of these dimensions of human existence. Further, all of these dimensions are necessary to the human vocation, God's calling upon us, to live on this planet as the image or reflection of God. The Second Adam, the Last Adam, has come to renew us in our human capacities and calling, not to remove them from our hands.

5
SANCTIFICATION AS RENEWAL IN LOVE

This is my commandment,
that you love one another as I have loved you.
—John 15:12

The gospel of Christ knows of no religion but social;
no holiness but social holiness.
—John Wesley, Preface to *Hymns and Sacred Poems* (1739)

OUR EXPLORATIONS of Christology in chapter 4 lead naturally and inevitably to a new batch of questions, such as: How do the theological battles fought by the likes of Irenaeus, Gregory, and Maximus bear upon our lives now—if they do at all? What difference does it make if, indeed, the Word of God truly became a full-fledged human being and lived among us on this planet twenty centuries in the past? How does the incarnation of God in Christ work to renew us in the image of God? Can such a renewal really draw us into renewed relations—not only with God and our fellow human beings but also with God's good creation? How much renewal can we realistically hope for in this life, under the conditions of human existence as we experience it today? To recall and adapt the question Gregory of Nazianzus posed, How does all this touch us now?

To help us wrestle with these questions, we turn to the ministry of John Wesley (1703-91) and his brother Charles (1707-88), Anglican priests who played a formative role in the eighteenth-century Methodist revival movement in England. Together, they wrote virtually countless prayers, sermons, and poems proclaiming the redemptive power of God through Christ in the Spirit. As we begin to address the above questions, the following lines from a poetic prayer written by the Wesley brothers, titled simply "Grace before Meat" (or what we might today paraphrase as "a mealtime prayer") may prove especially pertinent. The opening stanzas offer a candid confession of human sinfulness, rooted deeply in idolatry, and of the ways in which our diseased and distorted relations to fellow creatures are poisoning both ourselves and all of God's creation:

> *Enslaved to sense, to pleasure prone,*
>   *Fond of created good;*
> *Father, our helplessness we own,*
>   *And trembling taste our food.*
>
> *Trembling we taste: for ah! no more*
>   *To Thee the creatures lead;*
> *Changed, they exert a fatal power*
>   *And poison while they feed.*
>
> *Cursed for the sake of wretched man,*
>   *They now engross him whole;*
> *With pleasing force on earth detain*
>   *And sensualize his soul.*
>
> *Groveling on earth we still must lie*
>   *Till Christ the curse repeal;*
> *Till Christ, descending from on high,*
>   *Infected nature heal.*[1]

The clear message of this prayer is that we have lost our Way. Having fallen away from our original status, identity, and calling as creatures made in the divine image, we are out of harmony with God and with all God has made: "No more to Thee the creatures lead." Simply put, this prayer's language of *healing* inevitably assumes some prior loss or failure. *Sin* is the name given to this failure and loss. The biblical doctrine of sin, particularly as developed by the apostle Paul, teaches that "all have sinned and fall short of the glory of God" (Rom. 3:23). Indeed, in the same letter Paul describes human sin most fundamentally in terms of idolatry—"fond of created good," in the Wesleys' words—for we "exchanged the glory of the immortal God for images resembling a mortal human being or birds or four-footed animals or reptiles" (1:23).

To be sure, human beings, birds, four-footed animals, and reptiles are all good creatures of the good and holy God; there is nothing wrong, and everything right, about being any one of them. And we should be wary of language that simply dismisses or condemns any "fondness" for creation's blessings, joys, or pleasures. There is a proper delight in earth's creatures, a delight that Christian faith upholds and encourages. There is a proper curiosity that drives our efforts to understand the world better and to live in it more wisely. The problem arises when we refuse to see any divine reality beyond and through the creatures we encounter in this world of ours. Thus, while God intends creation and its wonders to bear testimony to the Creator (Ps. 19:1-4), human beings have refused and short-circuited this testimony. We have fixated upon the goods and beauties of creation—for they surely are good and beautiful!—and have not acknowledged their Creator in gratitude and worship. "Love the creature as it leads to the Creator,"[2] John Wesley counseled, but humanity has been universally content simply to love, worship, and serve creaturely goods. If this was true in Paul's time, and in Wesley's, how much more in our own? Consumerist culture thrives on this idolatry toward creation's goods, our economies driven by the power of media advertising that blatantly creates false needs and imaginary satisfactions.

In the face of our universal failure to love God, capitulating instead to idolatry, the Wesleys' mealtime prayer directs us to call upon Christ as the healer of all "infected nature." In his sermon "The Image of God," Wesley proclaimed our "merciful, though rejected, Creator would not forsake even the depraved work of his own hands, but . . . offered to him a means of being 'renewed after the image of him that created him.'"[3] And so the question lingers: How, and to what extent, can we be renewed in the image of God? Can our relations to God, to one another, and to all of God's creation be redeemed?

The Resurrection of the Incarnate Word

In the final stanzas of their mealtime prayer, the Wesleys begin to answer such questions; they encourage us to invite "our heavenly Adam" to come to us and "give [his] healing influence":

> Come then, our heavenly Adam, come,
> Thy healing influence give,
> Hallow our food, reverse our doom,
> And bid us eat, and live.
>
> Turn the full stream of nature's tide;
> Let all our actions tend
> To Thee their source; Thy love the guide,
> Thy glory be the end.
>
> Earth then a scale to heaven shall be;
> Sense shall point out the road;
> The creatures all shall lead to Thee;
> And all we taste be God.[4]

The Wesleys' language of the "heavenly Adam" comes from 1 Corinthians 15, one of several New Testament passages in which Paul draws the Adam-Christ contrast so formative for Irenaeus's recapitulation theory. Paul, drawing upon Genesis 2, writes that just as "the first man, Adam, became a living being" when God breathed into his nostrils the *ruach* of life, so "the last Adam became a life-giving spirit" (1 Cor. 15:45) when God raised him from the dead by the power of the Spirit of life. It is Jesus Christ as "the last Adam" (or "heavenly Adam" [cf. v. 49]) whom the Wesleys invoke in their prayer. It is crucial, though, to remember that the "heavenly Adam" has indeed already come to us decisively, and thoroughly, in the incarnation: *God in Christ truly has come to us*, in and among us, as one of us—a real human being of body, mind, and will.

Beyond the incarnation, Paul proclaims that the resurrected Christ, the "life-giving spirit," draws near us again. But the phrase "life-giving spirit" may sound troublesome. Was Christ's resurrection the undoing of the incarnation? Surely not! Paul's language should not be interpreted to imply that Christ has left behind the bodily existence of the incarnation, even though Paul does describe Jesus's (and our) resurrection body as a "spiritual body" (15:44). Of course there is this critical question, What is a "spiritual body"? No one really knows, though it is certainly possible that Paul has in mind some of the gospel descriptions of the resurrected Christ: his body bore the wounds of the crucifixion, and yet he was not always immediately recognizable (Matt. 28:17; Luke 24:16) and could mysteriously appear and disappear (Luke 24:31). There is both continuity and discontinuity between the earthly body and the resurrection body. In any case, Paul refuses to surrender the word concept of body (Gk., *soma*), for the body is created, sustained, cherished, loved, and resurrected by God.[5]

The point here is that Jesus's resurrection did not undo or reverse his incarnate existence; this underscores the crucial truth that the Christian doctrine of salvation is not a matter of "souls" or "spirits" being airlifted from God's good, material creation. The resurrection of the body validates the permanence of the incarnation, which in turn reinforces the goodness of the material creation. Thus, the "heavenly Adam" whom the Wesleys invoke is still Jesus the Nazarene, the Word Incarnate. If he comes to us as a "life-giving spirit" in the very presence and power of the Holy Spirit, he nevertheless comes in and with all of his truly lived history as a first-century Jew who "suffered under Pontius Pilate, was crucified, dead and buried."[6]

Thus, the same Jesus whom the church wrestled long and hard to affirm to be fully and truly human (as described in the previous chapter of this book) is the one who comes in the Spirit to us today. It is this "heavenly Adam" whose "healing influence" is given to us and to all creation. Toward what end does Christ's healing presence influence us? That end, or purpose, is "the new self, which is being renewed in knowledge according to the image of its creator" (Col. 3:10). Stated differently, the ultimate goal of Christ's healing influence[7] is our sanctification—which, in John Wesley's words, is nothing more or less than "the pure love of God and man; the loving God with all our heart and soul, and our neighbor as ourselves . . . love governing the heart and life, running through all our tempers, words, and actions."[8] It is God's love through Christ, in the Spirit, flowing into us and through us toward all that God has made and is making. This pure love of God and all neighbors necessarily occurs within the material world of creation. Thus, if divine love runs through "all our tempers, words, and actions," then this love must include our actions that have a direct bearing upon health and sustainability of God's material creation.

In their testimony to the "healing influence" of Christ, it is apparent that the Wesleys simply assumed, and built upon, the much earlier christological reflections of people like Irenaeus and Gregory of Nazianzus whose work we described in the previous chapter. This is evident in "Grace before Meat" and many other writings. They did not reinvent the christological wheel. Thus, there is comparatively little in their writings that explicitly connects the rich and dense incarnation of the Word to the renewal of humanity in God's image. They appear simply to have taken this critical idea for granted. From many of their sermons and poems, it becomes clear that their interests lay more in exploring how the Incarnate Word actually can and does touch us, and transform us, in the present. Their emphasis, then, falls upon the gift of the Holy Spirit, God's own dynamic, life-transforming Presence who enables us to cry out to God, "Abba! Father!" (Rom. 8:15-16; Gal. 4:6).[9]

Of course, it was that very prayer of Jesus in the garden of Gethsemane—*Abba! Father!* (Mark 14:36)—to which Maximus the Confessor and others appealed as support for a robust affirmation of Jesus's full humanity. The Christ of Gethsemane was "grieved and agitated"—indeed, "deeply grieved, even to death"!—and "threw himself on the ground" in agonizing prayer. In Gethsemane we encounter Jesus's own uncertainties and fears, and a frank acknowledgment of his own will and desires (Matt. 26:37-39). As we argued in chapter 4, without a full and honest acceptance of this portrait of the Second Adam in this second garden, we treat Jesus's obedience far too lightly and thereby refuse his deep and true sharing in creaturely realities. To do this, however, is to refuse the way of renewal through which our Maker has chosen to draw near to us in redeeming love. Hebrews reminds us, "In the days of his flesh, Jesus offered up prayers and supplications, with loud cries and tears, to the one who was able to save him from death, and he was heard because of his reverent submission" (5:7). But his "reverent submission" means nothing if it was simply automatic. The virtue of Jesus's obedience arises precisely because it was a *real obedience*, and thereby a faithful recapitulation of the purposes for which God has created human beings. In Jesus Christ we affirm (and more importantly, *God* affirms) the human body, the human mind, and the human will. In principle, then, Christians believe that "all things appertaining to the perfection of human nature"[10] were taken up into the divine life of the Incarnate Word and thereby healed. If the Wesleys' invocation of the "heavenly Adam" to "heal infected nature" rings true, then there is in Christ also a true renewal of our calling, and our capacity, to reflect God's character of outpoured love toward our fellow creatures.

In the light of these considerations, when the apostle Paul writes that "God has sent the Spirit of his Son into our hearts, crying, 'Abba! Father!'" (Gal. 4:6), we are in a position to understand the Holy Spirit as the Spirit of that faithful and obedient Son who in Gethsemane prayed that very prayer. The Holy Spirit communes with us and within us, such that the incarnate life of Jesus—his own struggles, temptations, prayers, and, finally, victory—is the life that God's Spirit bestows upon, among, and within us. This remarkable idea is implicit in the Wesleys' untiring emphasis upon the work of the Holy Spirit in our hearts and lives. For it was in the life, power, and love of the Spirit that Jesus himself prayed in the garden of Gethsemane and beyond as he trod the rough road of betrayal, trial, persecution, and crucifixion; as Hebrews puts it, "Christ . . . through the eternal Spirit offered himself without blemish to God" (9:14). That very Spirit of Christ, who offered himself so fully to God, is outpoured into our hearts. The Spirit gathers and empowers a people called the church to have "the mind which was in Christ, . . . walking as Christ also walked."[11]

If the Spirit whom God outpours upon us and within us is indeed the *Spirit of the Word Incarnate*, then we should not be surprised if God were to continue to touch us through material, fleshly realities. Our God is the God of incarnation. The Spirit of the One who cried out to God in Gethsemane encounters us incarnationally. But how does the resurrected Christ, the "heavenly Adam," touch us now? How might such renewing encounters occur?

"Renewal in the Image of God" through the Incarnate Word

We are arguing that for the Wesleys, and for the Wesleyan tradition after them, the lasting effects of the incarnation of the Word can and should deeply touch us, and transform us, today. The Wesleys placed a particularly strong emphasis upon the doctrine of humanity created in God's image—and of the real possibility of *renewal in the image of God*—in their understanding of salvation through Jesus Christ in the power of the Holy Spirit. In other words, the Wesleys maintained high hopes for what God's redeeming grace is able to accomplish for, in, and through human lives in this present world; for them, and for the Methodist movement they helped to lead, the power of sin can be overcome and human beings can indeed be restored *in this life* to living in God's image. Of course they were not (and are not) alone in this emphasis, but it is arguable that under their leadership the Wesleyan tradition has developed an especially robust understanding of salvation as *renewal in the image of God*. It is clear as well that Colossians 3:10—which speaks of a "new self, which is being renewed in knowledge according to the image of its creator"—provided the Wesleys with a compelling biblical warrant for their rhetoric of renewal.

The Wesley brothers' emphasis upon renewal in God's image ought to help us to appreciate, yet again, the idea that the doctrine of salvation is concerned not simply with "going to heaven when we die." Far more profoundly, salvation through Jesus Christ raises our sights about the kind of life we can live here and now, in this world, through the renewing grace of God. Salvation is not a divine rescue from the trash heap. If our lives can be renewed, it is because all creation can be renewed—and if that is so, it is because the Creator of all things wills and intends its renewal. This realization should help to underscore important biblical teachings about the goodness and redemptive possibilities of this material creation in the eyes of its Maker (1 Tim. 4:4; 6:17). Life in this world is not simply a place to wait for the next, nor is it a realm from which we long to escape, even if occasionally we hear sermons and hymns that suggest as much. John Wesley addressed the issue explicitly in the introduction of his classic sermon "The Scripture Way of Salvation":

> What is salvation? The salvation which is here [in Eph. 2:8] spoken of is not what is frequently understood by that word, the going to heaven, eternal happiness. It is not the soul's going

to paradise, . . . not a blessing which lies on the other side of death; or, as we usually speak, in the other world. . . . It is not something at a distance: it is a present thing; a blessing [offered] through the free mercy of God, . . . so that the salvation which is here spoken of might be extended to the entire work of God, from the first dawning of grace in the soul, till it is consummated in glory.[12]

Let us highlight Wesley's insistence that salvation is "not a blessing which lies on the other side of death; or, as we usually speak, in the other world." Obviously, if salvation lies not in "the other world," it is because salvation is a life intended for this world, beginning with "the first dawning of grace in the soul." Even when preaching in another sermon about the final judgment—where perhaps it might have been easy simply to try to scare people into getting their ticket to heaven punched—he still emphasized the idea that salvation is the Christian's journey "by faith to spotless love, to the full image of God renewed in the heart."[13] This is a journey to be taken in this life, while we live here on planet Earth.

What would such a transformation, such a journey, entail? Let us sample a few passages devoted to *renewal in the image of God* in John Wesley's preaching. In his 1736 sermon "The One Thing Needful," he insisted that God's fundamental goal for humanity— the "one thing needful"—"is the renewal of our fallen nature. In the image of God man was made . . . but sin has now effaced the image of God."[14] God's purpose both in creating us and redeeming us is that we might truly reflect or "image" our Creator within the realm of creation; therefore, this renewal in God's image is "the one end of our redemption as well as our creation."[15] Similarly, in the sermon "Original Sin" Wesley proclaimed that "the great end [or purpose] of religion is to renew our hearts in the image of God."[16]

But again we ask, How does this renewal occur? How does the Incarnate Word actually touch us? Wesley offers his most important reply in his sermon "The Means of Grace." Our Creator has given us practices such as prayer, corporate worship, reading the Scriptures, and the receiving the sacraments from the hands of others so that we, by grace, might attain "a heart renewed after the image of God."[17] This pronounced emphasis upon the means of grace should lead us to appreciate the incarnational nature of the Spirit's transformative presence and labor in our lives. Even while God the Spirit remains free to labor in unexpected and mysterious ways, the Wesleys assumed that the practices and sacraments of the church are "the ordinary channels of conveying [God's] grace into the souls of men." Sacramental practices—the waters of baptism, the bread and the cup, all received in company with other bodies who together compose one living sacrifice (Rom. 12:1-2)—reinforce and celebrate the goodness of God's material, bodily creation.[18]

The Wesleys did not think that the Holy Spirit just magically zaps us out of nowhere; on the other hand, they did not think that the Spirit was restricted to laboring only through the means of grace. Most assuredly, God in Christ by the Spirit is free to bestow renewing, healing grace in utterly unexpected ways and circumstances. Similarly, we ought not to assume a mechanistic or magical understanding of the means of grace, such that they just automatically dispense spiritual benefits. Nonetheless, the Wesleys encourage us to expect God to work through everyday means of grace—such as the reading and hearing of Scripture, personal and corporate prayer, relationships of encouragement and accountability, and regular participation in the Lord's Supper—to draw us into the orbit of divine grace embodied in the Incarnate Word, Jesus Christ. God "knows how we were made; he remembers that we are dust" (Ps. 103:14)— and God draws near to us accordingly, in ways that we can touch, taste, and feel (Ps. 34:8; 1 John 1:1-2). "Let all, therefore, who truly desire the grace of God," preached John Wesley, "eat of that bread, and drink of that cup."[19]

Our argument is that, for the Wesleys and the Wesleyan tradition, it is far too narrow to conceive of salvation simply as the forgiveness of sins so that we may gain entrance to heaven someday. Salvation properly understood is "full salvation," which means a salvation that brings *salving* or healing, true restoration and renewal, fully to human lives. All aspects and dimensions of human existence, nestled deeply within the complex manifolds of God's good creation, are to experience God's healing touch in the Word that became flesh and dwelled among all of us creatures. This implies a healing of all our relations—a healing that draws us increasingly into the reality of God's eternal love. This is nothing less than our sanctification.

The Image of God as Love

What did all this mean for the Wesleys and their fellow early Methodists? What did they believe that such a healing through Christ entailed? What is the image of God for which we were created and toward which we can be renewed?

Most fundamentally, God's original intention for human beings can be summed up with the term "love." For the Wesleys, the simple proclamation of 1 John that "God is love" (4:8, 16) was the central and controlling scriptural truth regarding God's character. Accordingly, they taught that the basic purpose of human life was to represent (*re*-present) and reflect God's love within the realm of creation. This theme in the Wesleys' theology connects powerfully with the ideas explored in this book's second chapter, "In the Image of the Social God." Consider for example John Wesley's rhetoric in his sermon "The Image of God," where he wrote that, in the beginning, "[humanity's] affections were rational, even, and regular—if we may be allowed to say "affections," for properly speaking he had only one [affection]: man was what God is, Love. Love filled the whole expansion of his soul; it possessed him without a rival. Every movement of his heart was love: it knew no other fervor."[20]

We should observe, first, that it is easy to suspect this sermon of overstating the case for original human perfection, even if we think simply in terms of the perfection of love. There is really nothing in

Genesis to encourage such strong, unqualified descriptions of humanity in the beginning—that from the very outset humanity *was* what God *is*: purely love. It would be better, we think, to interpret John Wesley's description of Adam and Eve in Eden as more the ideal to which humanity is called than as a perfection from which humanity has fallen. But even putting it that way is probably too strong. In traditional Christian teaching, the ideal for humanity is really never identified with Adam at all but with Jesus; in the words of Paul, Adam is but "a type of the one who was to come" (Rom. 5:14). In Jesus Christ we confess and believe that true human nature is unveiled; Jesus is the "last Adam," the Eschatological Human. This means that Jesus is the *telos*, the true goal and fulfillment of creation, the ultimate revelation of human existence as intended by God (cf. 1 Cor. 15:45-47).[21] We are led to confess that "God is love" not by the life of Adam in Genesis but by the self-giving life of Jesus who "laid down his life for us" (1 John 3:16). There is precious little in Genesis that would even begin to suggest such love in the lives of our earliest parents.

Even so, we acknowledge that Wesley tended to describe earliest humanity in grandiose imagery; he continues in "The Image of God":

> Love was [the human's] vital heat; it was the genial warmth that animated his whole frame. And the flame of [love] was continually streaming forth, directly to [God] from whom it came, and by reflection [from the human] to all sensitive natures, inasmuch as they too were [God's] offspring, but especially to those superior beings who bore not only the superscription, but likewise the image of their Creator.[22]

Even if we do question such exuberant speculations about the perfections of Adam, we can still appreciate that in this description we uncover the fundamental point in a Wesleyan theological anthropology (or the doctrine of what it means to be a human being created by God and in God's image). God is love, and human beings are created by God to be creatures from whom "the flame of [divine love] was continually streaming forth"—streaming back toward God, its Source, and thus also inevitably streaming forth toward all that God has created—including, of course, all of our fellow human beings who bear "the image of their Creator." But note that Wesley assumes that this divine love is intended by its Eternal Source also to "stream forth . . . by reflection" from human beings "to all sensitive natures"—by which he clearly means all animals who experience any measure of pleasure or pain[23]—"inasmuch as they too were [God's] offspring." It is worth noting, and likely surprising, that Wesley here described nonhuman creatures as the "offspring" of God! He also characterizes nonhuman creatures as bearing "the superscription . . . of their Creator." God's handiwork is all over them; each creature's unique properties and abilities mark it as a divine signature. While Wesley's language may strike us as unusual, we ought at least to acknowledge that he was looking for a way to overcome the sheer dichotomy too much of Christian thinking has created between "humanity in God's image" and everything else being, essentially, background noise. To his credit, Wesley understood the human vocation to be deeply interconnected with the more-than-human world. In the chapter to follow we will explore, in more detail, similar ideas in another of Wesley's sermons.

The main point for now is that the Wesleys offer us a remarkable description of God's intention for human beings: we are created to reflect or "image" God's love back toward God, toward all fellow human beings, and even beyond humans toward "all sensitive natures." This, for the Wesleys, is what it means to be human. God who is Eternal Love Streaming Forth has created us to receive this Love that is God's very reality, to return that love toward God, and to reflect that love toward all of our fellow creatures—together refracting God's love in every direction through all aspects, experiences, and relationships of our lives. Creation is intended by God to be a great and beautiful kaleidoscope of divine love.

It is no surprise, then, that in "Upon Our Lord's Sermon on the Mount, Discourse I" John Wesley rhetorically asks, "What is righteousness, but . . . the image of God stamped upon the heart, now renewed after the likeness of him who created it? What is it but the love of God, because he first loved us, and the love of all mankind for [God's] sake?"[24] Righteousness, or holiness, is the human heart and life renewed in God's likeness, which is immediately identified with self-giving, other-receiving love. In the light of our reading of Genesis 1, it seems unavoidable that God intends this divine love to be reflected toward creation and all of its manifold creatures.

We can further illustrate his point by noting that in his very early sermon "The Circumcision of the Heart" (1733), John preached to his Oxford listeners that holiness is "being so 'renewed in the image of our mind' as to be 'perfect, as our Father in heaven is perfect.'"[25] Here Wesley draws upon Jesus's words to his disciples in the Sermon on the Mount; it is crucial to consider the immediate context of these words (Matt. 5:43-48). Jesus has just observed that whereas human beings tend to love those who love them back, God loves all—the good and the evil, the just and the unjust. Jesus appeals to the evidence of nature to substantiate his message that God loves all people unconditionally: the blessings of sunshine and rain flow indiscriminately to everyone (v. 45). Likewise, Jesus's disciples are called to love not only their neighbors but also their enemies—and this is precisely the substance of what it means to "be perfect, therefore, as your heavenly Father is perfect" (v. 48). It is the perfection of divine love.

This idea that human beings can be renewed in the image of God who is Love, such that holiness is a "renewal in love,"[26] is probably most thoroughly explored in John Wesley's sermon "The One Thing Needful," which was cited earlier in this chapter. The one true necessity of human existence, he proclaimed, is "to be formed anew after the likeness of our Creator" because "love is the very image of God: it is the brightness of his glory. By love man is not only made like God, but in some sense one with God."[27] We become like God precisely to the extent that we receive through Jesus Christ the renewal of our nature in God's love. The sermon draws upon Romans 13:8 to argue for love's utter centrality: "The end of his commandment, too, was only our health, liberty, perfection, or, to say all in one word, charity. All the parts of [God's law find their] center in this one point, our renewal in the love of God."[28] Renewal in the image of God is renewal in "love divine, all loves excelling" through Jesus Christ. Having been so freely given such love as this, Wesley preached that it should be "our one view in all our thoughts, and words, and works, to be partakers of the divine nature."[29] If the divine nature is most essentially love (1 John 4:8, 16), as the Wesleys insisted,[30] then to fulfill our calling as the image of God means for humans to participate in this Love that God is. How do we partake of the divine nature? Or, to ask the question differently, How do we participate in Love Divine? To participate is to receive fully through Christ, and to share freely in the power of the Spirit, the free-flowing love of the triune God.

The Threefold Image of God

One more consideration will help to round out our discussion of the Wesleys' understanding of humanity created in God's image, and of how (and to what extent) we may be restored in that image. It will also anticipate the particular emphases of the chapter to follow. In his sermon "The New Birth" (1760) John Wesley suggested that the concept of the image of God could be analyzed under three different aspects or expressions: the natural, the political, and the moral.[31] Let us look briefly at each of these aspects.

Under the category of the *natural image*, we find Wesley describing humanity as "a spiritual being endued with understanding, freedom of will, and various affections."[32] The natural image, then, refers to the capacities that we identify as relatively unique to human creatures, capacities that tend to distinguish us from the other species. Thus, for Wesley "the natural image" corresponds with our discussion in chapter 4 of Irenaeus's interpretation of Genesis 1:26 regarding humanity's creation "in the image of God": for Irenaeus, our creation in the "image of God" denoted the natural capacities that distinguish humans from other creatures.[33] Wesley further identified these capacities as abstract and comparative thought; the power of willing, that is, of being aware of the desires and drives that move us; and liberty, or the capacity for responsible choice when presented with meaningful options, particularly between good and evil. Interestingly, Wesley held to this notion of the "natural image" even when, as he grew older, he became less willing to draw a bold line between humans and other animals of higher intelligence in regards to such capacities as these.[34]

It may be at least mildly surprising that by the *political image* John Wesley did not mean that humans are political animals in the way we often use that phrase. Rather, in this case and context "political image" has to do with the human calling and function to exercise godly rule among all of the rest of God's creatures. The political image refers to the human as created and called by God to be "the governor of this lower world,"[35] reflecting most particularly the language of Genesis 1:26 ("have dominion") and Psalm 8:6 ("all things under [humanity's] feet"). Accordingly, it is specifically as the political image that we humans are called to be, in Wesley's words, "the channel of conveyance" between the Creator and all other creatures so that "all the blessings of God" should "flow through [us]"[36] to the other creatures. "Thus," writes contemporary Methodist theologian Theodore Runyon, "humanity is the image of God *insofar* as the benevolence of God is reflected in human actions toward the rest of creation. This role as steward and caretaker of creation presupposes a continuing faithfulness to the order of the Creator."[37]

Both of these aspects of the image of God—the natural and the political—bear important implications for this book's argument. But in the present chapter we have concerned ourselves primarily with the third aspect, the *moral image*: humanity's God-given and God-graced potential for godliness, or god*like*ness, as revealed in Jesus Christ. Citing the apostle Paul, Wesley argued that this moral image "is 'righteousness and true holiness.' In this image of God man was made . . . 'God is love'; . . . God is full of justice, mercy, and truth: so was man as he came from the hands of his Creator."[38]

Clearly, for the Wesleys the most important dimension of the image of God that is restored through Christ and "stamped upon the heart" is the moral—and at the very heart of this moral dimension is *love*. This is the love revealed in the truly human body, mind, and will of Jesus Christ, the Incarnate Word. Further, this is the love "poured into our hearts through the Holy Spirit that has been given to us" (Rom. 5:5). Presumably, however, this moral dimension does not exist independently of the other two. These three aspects of the image of God are not airtight; surely we may anticipate, for example, that a restoration of the human being toward wholehearted love for God and neighbor (the "moral") will have immediate ramifications for how such a restored person lives in relation to the more-than-human world of material creation (the "political"). In other words, if the moral image is essentially divine love, and if human beings can be restored or renewed in that love through Jesus Christ, then such a life of love must necessarily find expression in actual, practical, everyday relationships with all other creatures. We would enact our human calling and function to exercise godly rule so that "all the blessings of God" would "flow through [us]"[39] to the other creatures.

Put even more simply, the life of holiness must include careful reflection (a capacity associated with the "natural image") upon questions of how we may most effectively reflect the love of God to all of creation—and to every one of God's creatures (a responsibility associated with the "political image"). For "God is love"—and, as John Wesley loved to cite, "Love has been perfected among us in this: that we may have boldness in the day of judgment, because *as [God] is, so are we in this world*" (1 John 4:16, 17).

6
TENDING TO
CREATION'S CRIES

We know that the whole creation has been groaning in labor pains until now.
—Rom. 8:22

While "the whole creation groaneth together"
(whether men attend or not), their groans are not dispersed in idle air,
but enter into the ears of God that made them.
—John Wesley, "The General Deliverance"

IF GOD has opened the way to our renewal in the divine image through Jesus Christ in the presence and power of the Holy Spirit, how will this renewal be brought to completion? What is our Creator's ultimate purpose for creation in all of this? If our renewal through Christ in the Spirit ought to produce love for God, for all neighbors, and for all creatures loved by their Creator, what end for the world—what goal or ultimate purpose—should we be anticipating?

When we ask questions of this sort, we are engaging the issues of eschatology. The doctrine of eschatology is about hope in God's future for creation. Christian eschatology must always be deeply rooted in Jesus Christ, whose coming has initiated the renewal of creation. But how will this decisive renewal be fulfilled? If we assume that God has entrusted to human beings the collective vocation of reflecting God's character of love toward creation—a theme assumed and explored throughout this book—how might God bring about creation's full fruition in glory? Do humans play a role? And is our role indispensable?

The great twentieth-century Jewish philosopher Martin Buber suggested a slight, yet momentous, modification of the Lord's Prayer: "'Let your will be done'—is all [we say], but truth goes on to say for [us]: 'through me whom you need.'"[1] We may very well balk at Buber's nudge, but it is arguable that his alteration arises from a profound understanding of Israel's testimony regarding the God of the covenants.[2] If our Creator truly is a covenantal God, is it not possible that in the work of *re*-creating, of making all things new, God shall labor everlastingly through covenantal relationship? Might not God *choose* to "need" us?[3]

These are challenging questions! In this chapter we will begin to attempt to probe these eschatological quandaries with the continued help of John Wesley. Because his emphasis upon renewal in the divine image, or renewal in love, inevitably entails a strong recognition of the reality of human agency and responsibility, his eschatological reflections should prove enlightening. In particular, this chapter will provide a sustained conversation with two of Wesley's best-known sermons on Christian eschatology: "The General Spread of the Gospel" and "The General Deliverance."

Eschatological Hope and Human Agency

Wesley's biblical text for "The General Spread of the Gospel" is Isaiah's prophecy, "The earth will be full of the knowledge of the LORD as the waters cover the sea" (11:9). This passage is brimming with eschatological expectation, anticipating a messianic figure called "the root of Jesse" who will bring about peace, justice, righteousness, and faithfulness throughout God's creation. It is a passage embodying, and inspiring, a hope in God's good intention (in the poetic words of his brother Charles) to "new-create a world of grace in all the image of Thy love."[4]

Yet, Wesley's sermon does not begin in hope; indeed, he opens by lamenting, "In what a condition is the world at present!" "The world at present" was the world that Wesley, by now the eighty-year-old leader of the Methodist movement, described as "darkness, intellectual darkness, ignorance, with vice and misery"[5] covering the face of the earth. "Such is the present state of humanity," he proclaims, "in all parts of the world! But how astonishing is this, if there is a God in heaven! . . . Surely this is one of the greatest mysteries under heaven!"[6]

Wesley here struggles with the world's stubborn refusal to be a utopia, the stark facticity of its unanswered questions and unfulfilled hopes—to say nothing of the stark struggles of its creatures to live through hunger, sickness, predation, natural disaster, and human violence. This is surely no less true of our world than it was of Wesley's. The world was then, and is now, full of heartache and mystery, suffering and anguish. And our immediate future looks grim. The health of the world's forests, rivers, and oceans is rapidly declining, and water quality remains the primary cause of human health problems worldwide. More than 600 million people are expected to lack access to safe drinking water by 2015, while more than 2.5 billion people will lack access to basic sanitation.[7] As our planet appears on the way to hosting 9 billion people by 2050,[8] urbanization and consumption are set to inflict unprecedented levels of damage and degradation on the planet.

But there's more. The human family's growing demand for resources has doubled since 1966 and is putting tremendous pressure on the diversity of earth's plants and animals.[9] In the past fifty years the overall number of species on the planet has decreased by 30 percent—a vast diversity of creatures created and beloved by God—with an even more pronounced effect on the tropics (60 percent loss of species). This rapid loss of species is estimated to be between one thousand and ten thousand times higher than the natural extinction rate; this translates to between ten thousand and one hundred thousand species becoming extinct each year as a result of human activity. Humans currently harvest 50 percent more of the earth's resources than it can actually reproduce. Citizens of the United States are consuming those resources at a far higher rate than any other people—and it would be the height of presumption simply to interpret this as God's blessing of one nation over all others. Instead, our self-gratifying consumption carries within itself its own damning judgment—but, tragically, that judgment is affecting all of earth's creatures, human and nonhuman, and their generations to come.

It is not difficult to wonder where God could be, or what God is doing, amid so much gone wrong and going worse. And in his own time, Wesley was willing to wonder about that, at least for a moment: "How is it possible to reconcile this with either the wisdom or the goodness of God?"[10]

Important as this question is, Wesley appears unwilling to entertain it very seriously, or at least for very long, in this sermon. What bestows comfort "under so melancholy a prospect" as the world as we know it? His one hope lies in "the consideration that things will not always be so; that another scene will soon be opened."[11] Understandably, Wesley appeals to the eschatological vision, to a hopeful yearning for a new world brought about by the Creator and Re-creator of all things: a less troubled and troublesome world, a world in which faith in God is not problematized by ambiguity or apathy or pain, one in which religious differences are erased and theological arguments silenced by a universally self-evident knowledge of the Holy One. Wesley proclaims that God "will arise and maintain his own cause," such that "the loving knowledge of God, producing uniform, uninterrupted holiness and happiness, shall cover the earth, shall fill every human soul."[12] This is indeed a vision of hope!

But Wesley could also imagine a reader objecting, "Impossible!" He anticipated that some would say that it is "the greatest of all impossibilities, that we should see a Christian world! Or for that matter, a Christian nation, or city!"[13] The passing of two and a quarter centuries only adds greater weight to this objection. We have certainly gotten no nearer to having a Christian world since Wesley's era! In so many ways our world's future prospects seem bleak indeed. But Wesley's response to such despair is pertinent regardless of the passage of time. He replies, "On one supposition, indeed, not only all impossibility but all difficulty vanishes away. Only suppose the Almighty to act *irresistibly*, and the thing is done; yea, with just the same ease as when 'God said, Let there be light; and there was light.'"[14] The God of all creation surely could, in the blink of an eye, transform the world for good.

It may be significant that this is the one place in the sermon where Wesley uses the traditional term "the Almighty" to refer to God. If "the Almighty" were to become fully manifest as "Almighty," "to act *irresistibly*," then a new and ideal world presumably could be ushered in now, this very moment. If God were "to act irresistibly," then no one or no thing would have the power to resist God's omnipotent will. God could simply do a giant makeover and right all the world's wrongs in an instant: clean air, pristine water, plenty of good land, happy animals, righteous people (with all the evil ones consigned to the flames of hell!). Wesley compares such power to thoroughly redeem the world with God's power to create, the power of calling light itself to be—that is, the might of the Almighty.

What is fascinating, though, is that while Wesley briefly mentions this "supposition" of an irresistible act of God, he dismisses it immediately: "But then man would be man no longer; his inmost nature would be changed. He would no longer be a moral agent, any more than the sun or the wind, as he would no longer be endued with liberty, a power of choosing or self-determination. Consequently he would no longer be capable of virtue or vice, of reward or punishment."[15]

This is a fascinating point, worthy of careful consideration. Though very often our own ideas about the end of the world are based upon the notion of God acting irresistibly, overpowering all opposition, Wesley (at least in this sermon!) offers this intriguing note of caution: were God so to act to enforce a world of righteousness, then the human being would be human no longer. Our "inmost nature would be changed," for our God-given power of moral agency would be overruled, canceled out.

Given the fact that Wesley has immediately rejected the idea of God acting "irresistibly," why did he even bother to mention it? Perhaps because of its enduring fascination, its widespread appeal, its popularity among many of his presumed audience? Perhaps Wesley felt himself drawn to its scenario—even while judging it unacceptable. In any case, Wesley dismisses this eschatological scenario because he recognizes that, in it, the human vocation of being the image of God, of reflecting God's great love to all creation, would have been nullified and "man would be man no longer." It is obvious that Wesley finds such an annulment of human vocation to be theologically untenable.

Let us consider more closely Wesley's point in the context of this book's argument. If God truly has created human beings to function as the divine image in the world, that is, to "image" or reflect God's character within creation—and if an important aspect of that function is the human capacity for moral agency and its ensuing responsibility—do we have good reason to expect our Creator to cancel this calling? Do we not believe with Paul that "the gifts and the calling of God are irrevocable" (Rom. 11:29)? If so, then how can we also maintain the hope that "the earth will be full of the knowledge of the LORD as the waters cover the sea" (Isa. 11:9)? How shall God bring this about? As contemporary Methodist theologian Catherine Keller has commented upon Wesley's quandary, "If God ultimately overpowers the creation, even for the sake of the creatures' own 'restoration,' would this not violate the human creature's freedom to 'react upon' grace, either resisting or embracing it?"[16]

This is a critical question. Note again that Wesley in the space of a few sentences dismisses the sort of presuppositions about how God exercises power that generally dominate typical expectations of traditional Christianity for the world's end. For Wesley such an irresistible act of God would be a betrayal of creation, an undoing of the divine purpose in creating creatures of agency to begin with. This is consistent with his strong opposition to Calvinist teachings on individual predestination—that God unilaterally and irresistibly has elected, from eternity, certain individuals to be saved (and the rest to be damned). Wesley, following in the wake of Dutch theologian Jacob Arminius (1560—1609), insisted instead that God freely offers grace through Jesus Christ to all people, but that anyone may (and many do) resist God's loving overtures.[17]

The point is that there is a real and important correspondence here: If God has lovingly created, and lovingly respects, human agency and responsibility in regards to individual salvation, then it is at least coherent to assume that God chooses to operate similarly in regard to cosmic salvation. God moves toward creation in gracious love, but God's grace always desires and invites a creaturely response. This understanding of God's gracious love and empowering presence was portrayed perfectly in the incarnation of the Divine Word, Jesus Christ. In his life and ministry, we see both God's gracious initiative toward us *and* the properly faithful, obedient human reply.

In other words, God has created us in order to co-operate, co-labor, with us. This is the nature of our covenantal God. This is reminiscent of Irenaeus (whose Christology we encountered in chapter 4) when he wrote that God redeems us "by persuasion, as it is fitting for God to receive what he wishes by gentleness and not by force." In God's renewing labor through Jesus Christ, Irenaeus continues, "neither was the standard of what is just infringed, nor did the ancient creation of God perish."[18] By undertaking the route of incarnation, God has chosen the gentle way of humble yet healing immersion within creation, such that "the ancient creation of God" did not perish—was not undone or destroyed—but was in fact quietly sustained.

To put it simply by splicing Wesley with Irenaeus, were "the Almighty to act *irresistibly*" then in fact "the ancient creation of God [would] perish." God's creation would "perish" because it would no longer exercise an existence distinct from (or answerable to) its Creator; it would be utterly absorbed by divine power. This would be a tragic reversal of God's purposes, an undoing of the creative Word, *Let there be*. More specifically, the "ancient creation" of human beings as the image of God would "perish" because their agency—and thus their responsibility before the Creator for the well-being of creation—would be entirely annulled. Such an irresistible act of God would also seem to transgress "the everlasting covenant between God and every living creature of all flesh that is on the earth" (Gen. 9:16), which was rooted in the promise always to sustain creation's natural rhythms rather than to destroy them.[19] Human existence, after all—including our capacities for reflection, action, agency, and responsibility—is deeply weaved into those natural rhythms of creation. God has created human beings to reflect God's glory, which is God's great love; there is no indication that God desires to cut short our vocation. Indeed, the coming of the Christ as a human being among us, participating fully in the life of "flesh," reinforces and renews our vocation.

Wesley, then, criticizes the typical expectation of an eschatological display of irresistible divine power, calling it a "clumsy way of cutting the knot which we are not able to untie."[20] In other words, we ought not simply to expect that God will unilaterally and instantaneously wipe creation clean (or wipe it out!). While affirming with Scripture that some kind of consummation is yet to come, we must be mindful of the "knot" to which Wesley alludes. This "knot" is created by the tightly interlaced threads of human history, identity, destiny, agency, and responsibility—inescapably complex as those are—interwoven always already with divine presence, purpose, and power. This exceedingly complex "knot" is the very mystery of divine providence in creation. Wesley is right; we cannot untie the knot of divine power and creaturely (not simply human) agency. We may, however, possibly loosen the knot a little if we understand divine power most essentially to be the *empowering* of the creature. This is not an *overpowering* that would render the creature (human or otherwise) incapable of living, moving, and having actual being—and thus lacking integrity. Rather, divine power is a subtle yet real *sharing* of power, of being, with the creature.

We maintain that this notion of divine power not only coheres with the invitational *Let there be* encountered repeatedly in Genesis 1, but also with the ultimate revelation given to us in the person, words, and works of Jesus Christ our Lord. As we argued in chapter 4, the Christian confession that Jesus is "truly God" and "truly human" in perfect union is a deep affirmation of God's ultimate intention to labor *with* us, to collaborate with the creature, rather than to squelch or deny human nature, even in its frailty and vulnerability. "The Word became flesh and lived among us" (John 1:14). Whatever else divine presence and power may do, it does not displace or overwhelm the true agency of creaturely existence such as we humans experience. Indeed, that was the burden of the argument of Maximus the Confessor and of Gregory of Nazianzus before him.

Even if this consideration loosens the knot, Wesley is certainly correct that we are unable finally to untie it. This knot is the paradoxical relation between divine power and creaturely agency, between divine providence and human responsibility. We have no need, and ought to have no desire, to remove the paradox. In fact, we have argued throughout this book that it is God who has "tied the knot" with us, and indeed with all creation: first in that lovely invitation *Let there be*; then with Scripture's first covenant, with all creation and every creature; then in the covenants with the people of Israel; and finally, fully, supremely in the person and history of the Nazarene, true union of the divine and the human in faithful covenant. God has indeed tied the knot.

But this leaves us stewing in the question Wesley asks: "How can all [human beings] be made holy and happy while they continue *to be* [truly] human beings?"[21] Can God's will "be done on earth as it is in heaven" as long as human beings exercise the power of will? Can we legitimately add to the prayer, as Buber gently suggested, "through me whom you need"? Or perhaps will God, one day, tire of dwelling with creation in longsuffering love? Will God despair of the human project on earth? Will the day come when God will say, "Enough!"?[22] So we ask again: How does our traditional eschatological hope interact with the doctrine of humanity's creation in the image of God or with God's "everlasting covenant" with all creatures[23] or with God's ultimate covenantal deed in the incarnation of the Word?

How Will God Redeem Creation?

Despite the corner into which he appears to have painted himself, Wesley insists that "there seems to be a plain, simple way of removing this difficulty without entangling ourselves in any subtle, metaphysical disquisitions."[24] But in fact, Wesley has already led us into those disquisitions. Indeed, they are unavoidable. To have appealed to human nature, to agency and responsibility, as Wesley did is to have become entangled in metaphysics. And he is not finished. He proceeds immediately with what sounds like a suspiciously metaphysical proposition: "As God is one, so the work of God is uniform in all ages."[25]

We must interrupt Wesley mid-thought. He is about to elaborate on the idea that the way God has labored in the world's past should give us a good sense for how God shall work in the future, for how our Creator will very soon bring about a world "full of the knowledge of the LORD as the waters cover the sea." Thus, to repeat: "as God is one, so the work of God is uniform"—or essentially the same—"in all ages." Wesley assumes a consistency, a constancy, in God's faithful relation with, and labors within, creation.

Wesley attributes his belief in the uniformity or constancy of God's work "in all ages" throughout creation to God's *unity* ("as God is one"). But it does not seem outlandish to suspect that God's *character* may also play a significant role. That is, Christian faith is grounded in the conviction that Jesus Christ is the revelation of God's moral nature: God is sacrificial love, and thus God always and everlastingly acts consistently in love. Love is God's "rule" of action because God's very nature is love. As Wesley commented elsewhere, the Johannine claim that "God is love" is "intimating that [love] is his darling, his reigning attribute, the attribute that sheds an amiable glory on all his other perfections."[26] God loving is God being God. Thus whatever God has done, is doing, or shall do, all flows directly from this infinite heart of divine perfection—the "amiable glory" of love coursing through the unimaginably rich communion of the triune God.

Accordingly, Wesley counsels us *not* to expect a radical change in the manner and mode of God's creating and redeeming activity in the world. Further, he appeals to human experience of God's redeeming love to argue that "God's general manner of working" is gracious assistance rather than force. Love does not force its way; thus, God's way of laboring with creatures of dust is in "gracious assistance." God enlightens and empowers human understanding and affections, God does not delete or undo them. It is critical to appreciate that this gracious synergism (Gk., *syn* = "together"; *erg* = "work") between God and human creatures provided Wesley with a model not simply for divine-human interaction but for the entirety of the God-world relation. Here he recites his favorite quotation from Augustine, "[God] who made us without ourselves will not save us without ourselves"—a beautiful underscoring of Wesley's own hard-fought synergism. Indeed, Wesley calls it "one of the noblest [sayings] Augustine ever uttered."[27]

Wesley then amplifies his appeal to our experience of how God works in our lives. "May we not then conceive how [God] *will* work on the souls of human beings in times to come by considering how he *does* work *now*, and how he *has* wrought in times past?"[28] Oddly, Wesley seems to have missed the sizable problem his rhetoric has created: he began this sermon by agonizing over the sad state of the world in which he lived—a state which, presumably, owed much to the ways that "God does work now" and "how God has [labored] in times past"! So if our clue regarding how to anticipate God's future work of renewal takes its cues from how God has worked in the past, we might wonder how different that future will actually look. The lamentable mess in which Wesley found his world (and in which we find ours) would presumably be a function, more or less, of "how God has [labored] in times past." Even if the mess is largely a result of human sin, frailty, or error, is this not ultimately the Creator's doing?

Of course, we acknowledge that so much of what has gone wrong is traceable to human action and influence. But creaturely agency is, we believe, also God's will. Most traditions within Christianity, perhaps the Wesleyan tradition in particular, fundamentally affirm the reality of human volition to be grounded in the "pure, unbounded love" of God. It is our infinitely loving Creator's wisdom and will that has gifted us with this precious, yet dangerous, power. Will our Creator take back what has been given? And if not, shall God's will ever be done on earth as it is in heaven? This is the question confronting us.

Undaunted, Wesley continues the appeal to his audience's Christian experience:

> You know how God wrought in *your own* soul when he first enabled you to say, "The life I now live, I live by faith in the Son of God, who loved me, and gave himself for me." He did not take away your understanding, but enlightened and strengthened it. He did not destroy any of your affections; rather, they were more vigorous than before. Least of all did he take away your liberty,

your power of choosing good or evil; [God] did not *force* you; but being *assisted* by his grace you, like Mary, *chose* the better part.[29]

This exposition is a classic depiction of Wesley's doctrine of prevenient grace and underscores the difficulty of walking the tightrope he has woven out of "the knot which we are not able to untie." If "the work of God is uniform in all ages," and if "God's general manner of working" is not by coercion or almighty fiat but rather by enlightening, strengthening, and assisting, then Wesley has knotted a difficult tightrope indeed. God has no interest or desire in nullifying human understanding, affections, or liberty; God is covenantally and faithfully committed to laboring with us rather than apart from us or in spite of us. And, we should add once more, the fullest testimony to this divine laboring has been delivered to us in the incarnation of the Word, Jesus Christ—truly God *and* truly human. The Christian faith confesses that *God has truly come to us* as Emmanuel, God with us as a fellow human being of body, mind, and will. This is how God has come, and this is how God has chosen to redeem creation. Perhaps any other way would, to draw once more upon Irenaeus's phrase, cause "the ancient creation of God [to] perish."

Liberation for All Creation

Jesus "suffered under Pontius Pilate, was crucified, dead, and buried"—God's incarnate Word, God's redeeming presence in our midst. So the renewing love of God was, by all appearances, defeated. But God raised Jesus from the dead, and it is precisely because God is faithful—the Father revealed in the crucified and resurrected Jesus by the power of the Holy Spirit—that we may "hope against hope" (Rom. 4:18, NASB) for creation's full redemption. This, however, is not a hope always easily sustained. Even as we human beings are created and called by our Maker to live in the world as God's image, we know too intimately our deep failure. Creation is marred by human sin, greed, and rebellion. Even as we celebrate the healing labors of God through the Incarnate Son, creation is riddled by pain, waste, and frustration.

So many of our world's woes are caused by human ignorance, greed, and apathy! Humanity's continuing increase in population growth is likely to result in greater water and food shortages, exponential leaps in pollution, and a notable increase in climate change-induced disasters. As more and more developing countries urbanize and modify their lands (e.g., by redirecting rivers or decreasing floodplains), the demand for water for agriculture and industry will increase. Pollutants from unregulated farming and manufacturing create an added concern because little or no progress has been achieved in preventing, reducing, or controlling pollution of the marine environment in the past fifty years. More than 90 percent of water and fish samples from aquatic environments are contaminated by pesticides.[30] Further, rapid industrialization in nations like India and China—who are, after all, simply following in the wake of Western nations—leads to the grim expectation that greenhouse emissions will increase by about 60 percent worldwide between 2005 and 2030.[31] Though Paul's words were penned nearly two thousand years ago, they reverberate hauntingly with enduring pertinence: "We know that the whole creation has been groaning in labor pains until now; . . . for the creation waits with eager longing for the revealing of the children of God; for the creation was subjected to futility . . . in hope that the creation itself will be set free from its bondage to decay and will obtain the freedom of the glory of the children of God" (Rom. 8:22, 19-21).

This dramatic passage from Romans 8 has become increasingly important in contemporary theological reflections upon creation and God's saving intentions for it. It also provided the text for Wesley's justly famous sermon "The General Deliverance," to which we now turn. In many ways, this is a truly remarkable sermon; while Paul's imagery of a groaning creation has become widely cited in contemporary theologies of creation care, Wesley lived in a different world. It was certainly not the norm in late eighteenth-century preaching to attend to the idea that nonhuman creatures will enjoy the blessings of the age to come! As is the case so often in our day, even more in Wesley's: Christians tended to think of the good news of Christ as relevant only to human beings, and then usually only to human souls upon the body's demise. Indeed, Wesley often wrote and preached essentially that message. But here, attending closely to Paul's writing about the groaning creation, Wesley explored new ground: "Nothing can be more [plain]: Away with vulgar prejudices"—by which he meant the typical human prejudices against the notion that God would actually love and care about the suffering of nonhuman creatures—"and let the plain word of God take place." All of God's beloved creatures, Wesley preached, shall experience deliverance from their sufferings and be ushered into "glorious liberty—even a measure, according as they are capable—of 'the liberty of the children of God.'"[32]

And how shall such a grand "general deliverance" actually occur? It is important to note that in this sermon Wesley asserts a critical role for humanity, created in God's image—especially under the aspect of the "political image" (as described in the previous chapter of this book). After citing Genesis 1 and Psalm 8, Wesley observes that God created and called humanity to be the Creator's "prince and governor upon earth, . . . the channel of conveyance between his Creator and the whole brute creation."[33] But we have mostly failed, rather miserably, to be conveyors of divine blessings, love, and compassion to God's more-than-human world. We must admit that Wesley, despite all of his rhetoric about the possibility of renewal in the image of God, does not in this sermon hold out much hope for what God may accomplish through faithful human obedience. He envisions that the "general deliverance" shall be accomplished by God, and God alone.

We should ask at this point, though, whether it is coherent or faithful to expect that God shall dispense with the vocation with which we human beings have been entrusted. The burden of this book has been to argue that God has not retreated, and shall not retreat, from issuing this calling to us human beings. Instead, God's decisive and ultimate act of healing for humanity, indeed for all creation, has occurred through the true and full incarnation of the divine Logos. *This is how God has brought renewal, and continues to bring renewal, to creation.* As truly God, Jesus embodies divine life, healing, and renewal in the midst of a groaning creation; as truly human—body, mind, volition—Jesus enacts faithful and authentic obedience to God's will for creation's healing. All of humanity is beckoned by God, in the power of the Spirit, to renewal through Christ. But apparently God has no interest in forcing our compliance. If our Creator does not coerce any one human being into renewal, then it seems consistent, and likely, that God will not coerce creation as a whole. God has come to us in the person and work of Jesus the Messiah to renew humanity, and so also to renew the earth. God calls us, but does not force us, to a renewal of human nature "in knowledge according to the image of its creator" (Col. 3:10). This renewal in the image of God means a renewal of our divine calling to function as God's image or reflection within our tiny sector of God's vast creation, the earth.

Thus, Wesley proclaims that when "the whole creation groans, . . . their groans are not dispersed in idle air, but enter into the ears of [God who] made them"—and he adds, not incidentally, that God hears these cries whether or not human beings are listening. But the clear implication is that human beings should indeed be listening—and acting accordingly—for we were created to be the creaturely representatives of the Creator's listening ear. God's insistent call upon Cain—"Listen; your brother's blood is crying to me from the ground!" (Gen. 4:10)—surely reverberates in our hearts today. Are we listening for creation's cries, including the cries of the impoverished people who are inevitably the first ones to suffer directly the effects of environmental degradation? And beyond the cries of fellow human beings, perhaps we can begin to attune our ears to the cries of God's vast array of creatures—of "all that have sense, all that are capable of pleasure or pain, of happiness or misery."[34]

In and through Jesus Christ, we are being re-created, renewed, for this vocation: to be God's listening ears and loving hands. Indeed, near the end of the sermon Wesley makes precisely this application to his hearers' lives. Anticipating an objector's question, "'But what end does it answer to dwell upon this subject, which we so imperfectly understand?" Wesley offers three considerations:

1. If we can be convinced that the Creator's "compassion is over all that he has made," then we may perhaps come to believe, and embrace for ourselves, the truth that God "is loving to every human being" (Ps. 145:9—one of Wesley's favorite verses). If God loves all snakes, cockroaches, and mosquitoes, then *how much more* does God love each of us?

2. If God, in the age of "the glory about to be revealed to us" (Rom. 8:18), shall lavish healing, peace, and liberation upon all the creatures that now groan in agony, then we receive "a full answer to a plausible objection against the justice of God,"[35] that is, the objection that God has allowed so much creaturely suffering in the world. It is noteworthy that Wesley considered the pains of animals to be worthy of theological attention; for him, it was not only human suffering that raised the specter of the problem of evil. "But the objection [against God's justice] vanishes away, if we consider that something better remains after death for these poor creatures also; that these, likewise, shall one day be delivered from this bondage of corruption, and shall then receive an ample amends for all their present sufferings."[36]

3. Most importantly for the argument of this book: if God is this kind of Creator—a God of compassionate love toward all creatures in all of their sufferings and satisfactions—then

human beings, created and called to "image" God, ought to stand up, take notice, and live accordingly:

> The preceding considerations [of this sermon] . . . may encourage us to imitate Him whose mercy is over all his works. They may soften our hearts towards the meaner creatures, knowing that the Lord cares for them. It may enlarge our hearts towards those poor creatures, to reflect that, as vile as they appear in our eyes, not one of them is forgotten in the sight of our Father which is in heaven. Through all the vanity to which they are now subjected, let us look to what God hath prepared for them.[37]

It certainly might be asked again, today, "But what end does it answer to dwell upon this subject, which we so imperfectly understand?" After all, did John Wesley really believe that all creatures that have ever lived and died on planet Earth would be resurrected into some (very large!) new world? Really? All the velociraptors who ever stalked the earth, to say nothing of alligators or snails or ants or pelicans? Can we really imagine such a thing, and does it serve any purpose to try?

But this is precisely where his third point becomes so important. We undoubtedly do not perfectly understand Paul's intentions in writing about creation's groans.[38] We cannot possibly imagine what God might have planned, if anything, for all of these creatures in some future world. But we certainly can comprehend the calling, already heard on the opening page of Scripture, that *adam* as male and female—all of humanity everywhere, at all times—is created and called by God to "have dominion over the fish of the sea and over the birds of the air and over every living thing that moves upon the earth" (Gen. 1:28). We have this calling—and since all those very creatures received a prior commission from the Creator to "be fruitful and multiply and fill the waters in the seas, and let birds multiply on the earth" (v. 22), we are again reminded that our "dominion" can only be intended for all these creatures' good.

Further, once we comprehend this "dominion" in the light of our *dominus*, our Lord Jesus Christ, we surely ought to be able to hear Wesley's sermonic injunction to "imitate [God] whose mercy is over all his works." If through Christ "the new self . . . is being renewed in knowledge according to the image of its creator" (Col. 3:10), then surely Wesley was correct to expect that a sermon like "The General Deliverance" should "soften our hearts," should "enlarge our hearts," toward all of God's creatures—feeble and frail creatures of dust. If in turn our hearts are indeed softened and enlarged toward God's creatures, then we must make practical efforts accordingly. Our renewal in God's image through Jesus Christ constrains us to reflect on how our selfish consumption of resources affects other creatures; it calls upon us to become more aware of the everyday choices we make (e.g., modifying our dietary patterns) because everything we do makes a demand on nature. If we each made some minor lifestyle changes—the food we eat, the clothes we buy, the way we travel—we could have a major impact on caring for God's creatures.

What Is God's "End" for the World?

While popular eschatology often obsesses about the end *of the world*, the argument of this book is to encourage us to live faithfully in the light of God's "end" or purpose *for the world*. What does God desire? What is our Creator intending? As Christians, we confess that God's supreme act of redemption has occurred in Jesus Christ; in that light, we confess, too, that the resurrection of the crucified Lord is the great sign of God's end for the world: life out of death, hope from ashes, light shining out of darkness (2 Cor. 4:6). It is patently obvious that the resurrection of Jesus did not bring about the end of the world; we are still here. Our planet is still spinning as it makes its annual journey around our life-sustaining star, within a vast galaxy that is itself on the move. Creation continues, and our Creator calls it all onward. Where are we all going?

Was Wesley correct to proclaim, "As God is one, so the work of God is uniform in all ages"? Would this sentiment preclude God doing a "new thing"? On the other hand, do we not believe already that God has done a great new thing in Jesus, such that "if anyone is in Christ, there is a new creation: everything old has passed away," that in Christ "everything has become new" (2 Cor. 5:17)? Are we willing truly to affirm this and to live in this new light of Christ? If God has performed the ultimate act of renewal of creation through the Incarnate Word who dwelled among us, as one of us, do we understand what it means to follow in the steps of this Divine Redeemer—body, mind, and volition? If he is himself the New Creation, is he touching us with its powerful, healing love?

Catherine Keller has rightly written that "surely no Wesleyan eschatology can well dispense with the new creation."[39] But it seems that we often are not terribly happy with the new creation with which we have been graced by God through Christ in the Spirit. Too often, perhaps overwhelmed by our own personal woes and those of the world, we long for the end. So we must ask again, What is the "end" that God desires for the world? A Wesleyan-shaped eschatology must fix its attention on what Scripture proclaims as God's ultimate intention for human existence: that we, and all people, might flourish ever more greatly and deeply in love for God and neighbor. Essentially, this is the meaning and goal of our having been created in God's image—along, of course, with the Genesis commission to reflect God's love, to re-present the covenantal character of the Creator, toward all of God's creatures.

What if we were to think of our local churches as communities who lived together faithfully under this calling to renewal in the image of God through Jesus Christ in the power of the Spirit? What if our life together corporately bore witness to the renewal of creation initiated in the incarnation of the Word? Interestingly, if we return to the Wesley sermon with which we began this chapter, "The General Spread of the Gospel," we find that Wesley actually pushed his hearers in this direction. He was convinced that the church could actually become the vanguard community of the age to come, a people whose life together bears witness to God's renewing love in Jesus Christ. Indeed, he believed, perhaps a bit naively, that his late-eighteenth-century Methodist movement was God's catalyst for transforming the world!—"All unprejudiced persons may see with their eyes," Wesley said of the Methodists, "that He is already renewing the face of the earth."[40]

Brimming with hope, Wesley anticipated that "all the inhabitants of the earth" would experience, in this life and in this world, God's great promises for creation: "They will not hurt or destroy on all my holy mountain" (Isa. 11:9). "Violence shall no more be heard in thy land, nor wasting nor destruction within thy borders."[41] For Wesley, such a world of peace and mutuality would be the direct result of "the general spread of the gospel" throughout the world through the faithfulness of God's people, the church. Sadly, we must admit that his optimism of grace now appears to have been vastly overstated. Yet we should ask: is this not still God's way of working? Do we have reason to think that God has abandoned this covenantal way, this collaboration with creation—not *forcing* us, but *assisting* us by grace, by the empowering presence of the Spirit? Could the church not yet be a community that proclaims, and embodies, God's renewal of creation in its worship, practices, and life together?

If Wesley is correct, it seems highly unlikely that God will force the world into being a place where "violence shall no more be heard in the land"—after all, would God act violently in order to abolish violence? Would our Creator violate the gift of freedom entrusted to humanity, or rob us of responsibility? All indications are that God's ultimate act of renewal, the person of Jesus of Nazareth, actually reinforces the role and responsibility of humanity as God's covenant partner. Thus, even as we acknowledge that Wesley's hopes were overblown, critical questions linger: Do we believe that God has actually begun a new creation through Jesus Christ, that the church is the community of new creation, and that we are therefore called upon to live in such a way as to bear witness to divine peace (Eph. 2:13-21)? And does that peace embrace all of creation, and all of God's creatures?

If we are willing to answer these questions with a *Yes*, then perhaps we are near to comprehending the divine *telos, God's true end* for the world. The new creation is always a creation of greater possibilities for love: for God; for all people, created to reflect God; and for all of God's creatures, all of whom exist within the infinite depths of divine compassion. "Your steadfast love, O LORD, extends to the heavens, your faithfulness to the clouds. . . . You save humans and animals alike, O LORD" (Ps. 36:5-6). This faithful, steadfast love is the very character of God; for human creatures, this love must be received, learned, and practiced. Perhaps for human love to exist, let alone to grow and thrive, it may require a world such as the one in which we live.

But if all our eschatological reasoning should fail, at the very least we might remember, with God, the rainbow—"the sign of the covenant that I make between me and you and every living creature that is with you, for all future generations" (Gen. 9:12).

Most assuredly, God does not forget rainbows.

PART III
Sabbath

7

GATHERING UP
THE FRAGMENTS
(A Sabbath Meditation)

*Now that day was a sabbath. . . . Jesus answered . . . ,
"My Father is still working, and I also am working."*
—John 5:9, 17

THE ARGUMENT of this book has laid considerable stress upon God's calling of human beings to reflect the reality and character of our Creator. Our creation in God's image means that we are beckoned to image or reflect the Creator throughout creation. This, we have argued, is the fundamental task entrusted to *adam*—which is to say, to all human beings everywhere and at all times. It is a weighty responsibility, a deadly serious vocation. Creation is groaning.

But Scripture also reminds us repeatedly that *we are only dust* (Ps. 103:14). We are finite, frail, vulnerable creatures. We are not God—even if we are created in God's image and called toward God's likeness. We are creatures who require rest, who need Sabbath's regularly repeated reminder that we are not God. "It is [God] who has made us, and not we ourselves" (Ps. 100:3, NASB). The Sabbath is a wonderful gift lavished first upon the Jewish people, and through them to all people, calling us to cease from our labors in the full confidence that the world ultimately belongs to God and spins under divine jurisdiction. Indeed, the Sabbath is also God's gift of rest to all of creation—the land, the animals, the plants, and the trees (Lev. 25:2-7). We are not carrying everything upon our shoulders. We are invited by the Creator to stop, to rest, to take a breather, to relax in the trust that "the earth is the LORD's, and the fulness thereof" (Ps. 24:1, KJV).[1] And we are called upon by the Creator to extend that trusting restfulness to all creatures and everything around us (Exod. 23:10-11).

The Jewish tradition has developed a beautiful theology of Sabbath that would instruct us, too, that this day of rest is an anticipation of God's future, a quickly passing yet weekly glimpse into the age to come. Creation's Sabbath pause encourages us to look forward to the new creation; indeed, Sabbath practices (such as lighting candles, singing praise to God, sharing in good food together) are intended to provide a real foretaste of creation's fulfillment, an everlasting day of rest and joy. Sabbath, accordingly, is a profoundly eschatological practice.

Inviting as that probably sounds, a critical question emerges. At least in some Christian circles, eschatological expectations can easily breed passivity—particularly when they are wrapped in predictions of a looming apocalypse, a divinely dramatic end to the world as we know it, believed to be right around the corner. Since the world is about to end, why should we care so much for its health or well-being? In fact, if Jesus is coming very soon, should we not expect that the world and its resources would be in crisis? For that matter, might it not be possible for us to hasten Christ's return by accelerating our devastation of earth's resources? For this unfortunate way of thinking, the bleaker the situation appears—whether a matter of environmental degradation or escalating tensions in the Middle East or the threat of a terrorist group getting its hands on a nuclear warhead—the more likely that Jesus's return is imminent.

Happily, this version of Christian eschatology appears to be on the wane. But it continues its destructive influence. In reply to this sort of defeatist, and escapist, eschatology, it may be useful in this final chapter, offered in the spirit of a closing meditation, to consider an intriguing passage from the gospel of John. It is John's version of the miracle (or "sign") of Jesus's feeding of the multitudes:

> Jesus went up the mountain and sat down there with his disciples. Now the Passover, the festival of the Jews, was near. When he looked up and saw a large crowd coming toward him, Jesus said to Philip, "Where are we to buy bread for these people to eat?" He said this to test him, for he himself knew what he was going to do. Philip answered him, "Six months' wages would not buy enough bread for each of them to get a little." One of his disciples, Andrew, Simon Peter's brother, said to him, "There is a boy here who has five barley loaves and two fish. But what are they among so many people?" Jesus said, "Make the people sit down." Now there was a great deal of grass in the place; so they sat down, about five thousand in all. Then Jesus took the loaves, and when he had given thanks, he distributed them to those who were seated; so also the fish, as much as they wanted. When they were satisfied, he told his disciples, "Gather up the fragments left over, so that nothing may be lost." (6:3-12)

There is no question that John's gospel (like the other gospels) encourages us to read this miraculous feeding in the light of the eucharistic celebration, the Lord's Supper. We recall that Jesus's "first sign" in John is the turning of water into wine at the wedding feast in Cana (2:1-11), so that with these two signs of Jesus we receive both the wine and the bread. Further, not only do we read that Jesus had given thanks before distributing the food (6:11), but that very point receives further emphasis later in the same chapter (v. 23) when John refers to "the place where they had eaten the bread after the Lord *had given thanks*"—the Greek verb is *eucharistisas*. When later in the chapter Jesus calls himself "the bread of life" (v. 35) and proclaims that "the bread that I will give for the life of the world is my flesh" (v. 51), the eucharistic references are unmistakable and mounting. "So Jesus said to them, 'Very truly, I tell you, unless you eat the flesh of the Son of Man and drink his blood, you have no life in you'" (v. 53). Here we encounter, in the words of biblical scholar Gail O'Day, "an affirmation of the incarnation of the Son of Man" coupled with "unmistakable Eucharistic associations."[2]

It is widely believed by biblical scholars that Jesus's feeding of the crowds should be interpreted also in the light of prophetic passages such as Isaiah 25:6-9, where God's great age to come is characterized as a joyful feast:

On this mountain the LORD of hosts will make for all peoples
a feast of rich food, a feast of well-aged wines, . . .
And he will destroy on this mountain
the shroud that is cast over all peoples,
the sheet that is spread over all nations;
he will swallow up death forever.
Then the LORD God will wipe away the tears from all faces,
and the disgrace of his people [Israel] he will take away
from all the earth,
for the LORD has spoken.
It will be said on that day,
Lo, this is our God; we have waited for him, so that he
might save us.
This is the LORD for whom we have waited;
let us be glad and rejoice in his salvation.

For the gospel of John especially, Jesus's person, ministry, and "signs" are all potent manifestations of the age to come. In him the judgment of God is already here (John 3:18-19). He is the Light that overcomes and dispels darkness. Most famously, when Martha testifies of her brother Lazarus, "I know that he will rise again in the resurrection on the last day," Jesus replies, "I am the resurrection and the life" (John 11:24-25). This sense of the "already but not yet" age to come courses throughout the gospel of John. It is surely present in the feeding of the multitude as well. *This is the eschatological feast for the nations*—and it is, not coincidentally, also the church's ongoing feast of the Eucharist. Further, to participate in the Lord's Supper is to receive a foretaste of the messianic banquet in the age to come; as Jesus said to his disciples at the table, "I will never again drink of this fruit of the vine until that day when I drink it new with you in my Father's kingdom" (Matt. 26:29; cf. Mark 14:25; Luke 22:16-18; 1 Cor. 11:26). Particularly in John's gospel, though, we find that the feeding of the crowd by the Sea of Galilee, the church's eucharistic meal, and the heavenly banquet of the age to come all tend to become blended beautifully, like images in a kaleidoscope, into one Table.

In chapter 4 of this book we have seen how the second-century bishop and theologian Irenaeus drew from scriptural imagery to weave deep and lovely connections between creation and incarnation, between the material and the spiritual, between bread from the earth and the Bread of Heaven. The Word has "become flesh and lived among us," one of us, declaring by his very living and doing, by his speaking and being, the transcendent God whom "no one has ever seen" (John 1:18). In Irenaeus's words,

> Although the Lord could have provided wine for the feasters and satisfied the hungry with food without using any object of the created order, he did not do so; but taking loaves which came from the earth, and giving thanks, and again making water into wine, he satisfied those who lay down to eat, and he gave drink to those who were invited to the wedding. Thus he showed that God who made the earth, and commanded it to bring forth fruit, and established the waters, and brought forth the springs, also in these last times through his Son gives to the human race the blessing of food and the favor of drink, the incomprehensible through the comprehensible and the invisible through the visible.[3]

God the Creator of all things has entered into the material goodness of creation through the incarnation of the Son, blessing us and re-blessing us with its goods. Thus we are bold to anticipate creation's full renewal and redemption.

But we reiterate that, from the perspective of John's gospel, this big meal on the Galilean hillsides is already in itself a sign of eschatological fullness, a realization of eschatological hope. The Son of God, the Resurrection and the Life, is already giving of his flesh and blood for the world. This is the arrival of the age to come! The Messiah is already now providing "a feast of rich food, a feast of well-aged wines" for all the peoples of earth (Isa. 25:6). Surely many in the crowd, perhaps especially Jesus's own disciples, would have believed this to be a sign of the end. Even if they did not believe this meal to be the messianic banquet in the fullest sense, they surely felt it was a taste of the great feast to come.

Who, then, among Jesus's disciples could have anticipated his simple instructions after the feast? "Gather up the fragments left over, so that nothing may be lost" (John 6:12). What? After this grand messianic meal? After this filling foretaste of the heavenly banquet to come, this Eucharist for thousands? Why worry about leftovers? If in Jesus Christ the resurrection and the life has fully arrived and dwells among us, all the nations are invited to the table; no one need ever go hungry again.

Why, then, does Jesus instruct his followers to "gather up the fragments"? It is easy to imagine the disciples wondering, "Jesus, can't you simply whip up another big feast tomorrow? Can't we do this every day? You are the Christ, the very Presence of the age to come, the Resurrection and the Life in the here and now! Just do another sign like this tomorrow—every day! You could turn water into wine and crumbs into loaves for every meal; it's Eucharist, and a whole lot more, every day into eternity!"

Some may insist that Jesus is coming soon, and that in the light of his imminent return there is no need to worry about the fragments.

Some Christians have argued that if the world as we know it is about to end, then we may as well use up its resources and get it over with. Too often popular eschatology operates on precisely these faulty assumptions. While the resurrection of Jesus Christ is God's wondrous guarantee that God's redemptive purposes shall be fulfilled, our Christian hope is not predicated on doomsday predictions about the world's demise. Instead, here is the Christ of the gospel of John, the Bread of Heaven, the Resurrection and the Life, quietly instructing his disciples, *Gather up the fragments, so that nothing be wasted.*

This is not to make Jesus into an ecologist, except perhaps in the broadest sense of the term. It seems likely that Jesus's instructions echo those of Moses to the Israelites as they gathered manna, that none of it was to be left out on the ground (Exod. 16:19-20). In both stories, there is an implied warning against taking God's provisions for granted or treating them lightly, as though God can always be counted upon to compensate for human wastefulness. Regardless of the range of possible meanings Jesus's instructions might have held for the readers of John's gospel at the end of the first century, for us they provide the bare seed, the humble beginnings, of a fundamentally Christian orientation toward the material goods of God's green earth. *Gather up the fragments.*

To *gather up the fragments* suggests humble acts. Fragments are small. They may not even appear edible. Apparently those fragments matter to Jesus, this One who turned water into wine and biscuits into banquets. To gather up the fragments is to take nothing for granted. It is to do the small thing, the fragmentary thing. It might be turning off lights when we leave a room. Or taking a shorter shower. Or taking less in the school cafeteria, and eating what we take. Or taking reusable bags with us to the grocery store.

The instructions *Gather up the fragments* suggest a certain sort of gentle care, of humble nurturing, of creation's goods. There is no encouragement here of extravagant waste, even in the presence of the Messiah who freely offers food and drink to all people. "But there is much more where that came from," his disciples undoubtedly thought to themselves. So it is not difficult to imagine their eschatology encouraging them to take a careless attitude toward creation's goods. Yet Jesus himself, the Resurrection and the Life, instructed them—*instructs us*—to *gather up the fragments, so that nothing be wasted.*

Gathering up the fragments may well even include picking up trash, especially plastics, to help insure cleaner land and oceans. Surely today it would include recycling and encouraging our local churches and universities to participate fully in recycling programs. It would include unplugging our electronic gadgets, and especially cords that are not in use. It means seriously rethinking our modes of transportation—might we walk or bicycle more regularly than we do or learn to rely upon public transportation rather than privately owned and maintained automobiles? Even closer to the story in John, it may entail participating in a community vegetable garden or helping to get one started at church.

Gathering up the fragments might move the members of a church youth group or university club to "adopt" a stretch of highway or several city blocks or a stretch of shoreline as their own corner of God's creation to keep clean, beautiful, and productive. Perhaps it could mean becoming involved in a local restoration project, participating with others in simple efforts to restore a lagoon or estuary to its native habitat for the well-being of native plants and animals. These are but a few of the small yet significant ways in which Jesus's disciples can faithfully obey his eschatological instruction, "Gather up the fragments."

The gospels instruct us that Jesus understood and practiced Sabbath as a day for doing good, for nurturing, healing, and saving life (Mark 3:4). It is undeniable that God's good earth is in need of some good to be done for it; indeed, as we have argued in this book, all of us, and all of our neighbors—human and nonhuman, present and future—fundamentally need a healthy planet in order to live, let alone to thrive.

Jesus was accused repeatedly of breaking the Sabbath. His reply, essentially, was that there is a hardhearted, calculating way to observe the Sabbath—but that there is also, and much better, a compassionate, healing way to observe the Sabbath that aims at creation's well-being. Even on the Sabbath, Jesus taught, "My Father is still working, and I also am working" (John 5:17); the Son, in turn, entrusts to his disciples a working, a sabbatical practice: *Gather up the fragments, so that nothing be wasted.*

May we, by the grace of God who calls us in Christ by the Spirit, respond in loving obedience. *Amen.*

THE EIGHTH DAY

And the leaves of the tree are for the healing of the nations.
—Rev. 22:2

Throughout this book we have explored the way God calls us to participate in the loving care of creation. This participation is at the heart of what it means to be created in the image of God. This working together of God and human beings finds its fullest expression in Jesus Christ, truly God and truly human, through whom fallen humanity receives renewal in the image of the One who is Love.

Rather than waiting for some catastrophic end to creation, as popular eschatology often maintains, we have acknowledged that humanity has much to do to fulfill its function of "imaging" God to creation. To image God means to image Love, and so humanity is to reflect this God of love to creation. This does not preclude our eschatological hope for creation's ultimate redemption through Jesus Christ, but it does insist that in the meantime we are called to a loving regard for all creation—human and nonhuman. We are not bystanders waiting for the end but participants living toward that end—God's graciously intended end for God's good creation.

If we consider the way God has worked in the past and continues to work now, in the light of his covenantal promises, we can conceive that God will work similarly in the future—the Creator and human creatures laboring covenantally for the final redemption of all that has been made. We know this to be true because we have already witnessed this divine-human cooperation in Jesus, God's Incarnate Wisdom, in whom this co-laboring has been revealed most dramatically and clearly.

In Jesus's life, crucifixion, and resurrection, we taste the fullness of redemption; through him is healing for all God's creation, but as the Scriptures attest, beyond the taste there is yet to come a full and ultimate feast. The object of the Christian hope—of full renewal for all creation, of the gracious restoration of life, of the ongoing participation of humankind in God's purposes in newer and more wonderful ways—that hope still awaits final fulfillment in a Sabbath of Sabbaths, a true messianic banquet in the age to come. During this present age may we engage ourselves wholeheartedly as co-workers with God, reflecting to all creation the One who has renewed us in his image—the One "whose last, best word is love."[1]

NOTES

Chapter 1

1. This is not to imply that the language of "the image of God" should not be interpreted within even larger contexts, such as, for example, Genesis as a whole or the Torah as a whole or even the Christian Bible as a whole, particularly as it is interpreted in the light of Jesus Christ. But we begin here somewhat humbly with Genesis 1 under the assumption that this narrative did function, at least to some extent and for at least a period of time, as something like a creation story in and of itself. To be sure, we certainly will attempt also to read it in the light of Christ.

2. For further study on this issue, see John H. Walton, *The Lost World of Genesis One: Ancient Cosmology and the Origins Debate* (Downers Grove, IL: InterVarsity Press Academic, 2009); and Tremper Longman III, *How to Read Genesis* (Downers Grove, IL: InterVarsity Press Academic, 2005).

3. As H. Orton Wiley so aptly described, and analyzed, Genesis 1 in his *Christian Theology* ([Kansas City: Beacon Hill Press, 1940], 1:449-54).

4. For an insightful treatment of the language of Genesis 1 in the light of current scientific models of the earth and its atmosphere, see Karen Strand Winslow, "The Earth Is Not a Planet," in *Creation Made Free: Open Theology Engaging Science*, ed. Thomas Jay Oord (Eugene, OR: Wipf & Stock, 2009), 13-27.

5. The "day-age" theory finds favor among interpreters who are convinced by geological evidence that the earth is far older than just a few thousand years but who also feel constrained to read Genesis 1 as a kind of scientific account. In order to make room in the text for a much older earth, they appeal to the fact that the Hebrew word *yom*, while typically translated by the English word "day," can also mean an unspecified "period of time." The great twentieth-century Nazarene theologian H. Orton Wiley, for example, tended to view this interpretive approach favorably; see his *Christian Theology* (1:466). It might be suggested that Wiley should have taken far more seriously his own characterization of Genesis 1 as the "Hymn of Creation" or the "Poem of the Dawn" (ibid., 449).

According to the day-age approach, any given *yom* of Genesis 1 could be interpreted to entail a considerably long period of time, rendering the account more amenable to an old earth and perhaps even, at least roughly, to an evolutionary description of the creation of living things on this planet. The point at hand, however, is that this interpretive model undergoes considerable strain if the third "day" is one of these very long periods of time. It would mean that God created all kinds of vegetation that thrived—for however long this *yom* might have been—without the benefit of the sun, yet to be created. If, on the other hand, it were to be objected that perhaps this particular *yom* was a very brief period of time, it would be difficult not to suspect a large dose of special pleading.

Even if the "day-age" theory is rejected, it seems safe to assume that the writer(s) of Genesis 1 did not know that earth's vegetation cannot survive without sunlight. This is not problematic as long as we do not expect Genesis 1 to function as a source of scientific information about the world.

6. Gerhard von Rad, *Genesis: A Commentary* (Philadelphia: Westminster Press, 1966), 53.

7. Again, see Walton, *Lost World of Genesis One*, especially "Proposition 2: Ancient Cosmology Is Function Oriented" and "Proposition 3: 'Create' (Hebrew *bārā*) Concerns Functions" (pp. 23-46).

Chapter 2

1. Indeed, *elohim* is translated as "gods" at least sometimes in the Old Testament, and Psalm 82:1 is a good example. It is noteworthy that the gospel of John quotes Psalm 82:1 to support Jesus's deity, "Is it not written in your law, 'I said, you are gods'?" (John 10:34). Psalm 8:5, discussed in the previous chapter, states somewhat surprisingly that human beings are made "a little lower than God [*elohim*]," translated sometimes as "God" and other times as "angels."

2. The Greek text of John 1:1 presents a fascinating detail. In the phrase often translated "and the Word was God," there is no definite article with "God." Given that lack of a definite article, the phrase probably would be better translated "and the Word was divine" or, in the even more preferable language of the *Revised English Bible*, "what God was, the Word was." The main point is that "the Word was God" can mislead a reader into the notion that the Word was simply identical with God, such that God and the Word are "one and the same." Such an idea undercuts the possibility of an "I-Thou" relationship between God and the Word. On the other hand, the Jehovah's Witnesses' *New World Translation* (copyright 1961, 1970, 1981, 1984, 2013 Watch Tower Bible and Tract Society of Pennsylvania) supplies an indefinite article to translate the phrase "and the Word was a god." This is generally believed by scholars to be a woefully unjustified translation of the Greek text—and also leads to a denial of Christ's full deity, a christological position condemned as heretical at the Council of Nicea (325).

3. This emerges most clearly in the apocryphal book of Wisdom, which is canonical for the Roman Catholic Church but not for most Protestant bodies. Nonetheless, it certainly gives its readers important insight into the ways that at least some Jews of roughly the time of Jesus, and before, were coming to understand Wisdom as God present and active in the world. For example, "She is a reflection of eternal light, a spotless mirror of the working of God, and an image of his goodness. Though she is but one, she can do all things, and while remaining in herself,

she renews all things; . . . She reaches mightily from one end of the earth to the other and she orders all things well" (Wisd. Sol. 7:26-27; 8:1).

4. Charles Wesley hymn, "Love Divine, All Loves Excelling," *Sing to the Lord* (Kansas City: Lillenas Publishing, 1993), 507.

5. See, for just one prominent example, Gerhard von Rad, *Genesis (Old Testament Library* series; Louisville, KY: Westminster John Knox Press, 1973), 58.

6. Ibid. Von Rad's gender-exclusive language of forty years ago should not blur the jolting fact that in Genesis 1, this "function in the nonhuman world" is bequeathed by God to *adam* or humanity as *"male and female."* Whatever is entailed in living in (or living as) the image of God, it is entailed of all women and men with no difference whatsoever mentioned by the text.

7. Eric Chivian and Aaron Bernstein, eds., *Sustaining Life: How Human Health Depends on Biodiversity* (Center for Health and the Global Environment; New York: Oxford University Press, 2008).

8. For further reading on this issue, see Ellen F. Davis, *Scripture, Culture, and Agriculture: An Agrarian Reading of the Bible* (New York: Cambridge University Press, 2009), 53-63.

9. For a fruitful exploration of this idea, see Terence Fretheim, *Creation Untamed: The Bible, God, and Natural Disasters* (Grand Rapids: Baker Academic, 2010).

10. von Rad, *Genesis,* 59. It may at least be possible to consider the practice of Christian vegetarianism to be a particular calling to which some in the body of Christ are called.

11. Augustine, *Confessions,* R. S. Pine-Coffin, trans. and intro. (London: Penguin Books, 1961), 302.

12. Ibid., 302-3.

13. Ibid., 303.

14. Augustine, *On Christian Doctrine,* translated with an introduction and notes by R. P. H. Green (Oxford, UK: Oxford University Press, 1997), 77, 76, 79.

15. "IPCC, 2014: Summary for Policymakers," at http://mitigation2014.org /report/summary-for-policy-makers (accessed May 12, 2014).

16. S. A. Ahmed, N. S. Diffenbaugh, T. W. Hertel, D. B. Lobell, N. Ramankutty, A. R. Rios, and P. Rowhani, "Climate volatility and poverty vulnerability in Tanzania," *Global Environmental Change* 21 (2011:1), 46-55.

Chapter 3

1. John Wesley, "The General Deliverance," *The Works of John Wesley* (Kansas City: Nazarene Publishing House, 1872 authorized ed. of the Wesleyan Conference Office), 6:244. Hereinafter referred to as *Works.*

2. In fact, since the Bible does not limit God's creative activity to the six days of Genesis 1, but proclaims God's ongoing labors as Creator of all things (e.g., Ps. 104; Isa. 43:14-21), it is reasonable and theologically responsible to assume that God continues the work of creation, in a timeful way, into this very present moment.

3. See M. Lodahl, "Knowing Noah—Or Not," chapter 7 in *Claiming Abraham: Reading the Bible and the Qur'an Side by Side* (Grand Rapids: Brazos Press, 2010), 113-26.

4. John Wesley, *Explanatory Notes upon the Old Testament* (Salem, OH: Schmul Publishers, 1975), 1:42.

5. See Ellen Davis, *Scripture, Culture, and Agriculture: An Agrarian Reading of the Bible* (New York: Cambridge University Press, 2008), 17-19.

6. Otto Kaiser, trans. R. A. Wilson, *Isaiah 13—39: A Commentary* (*The Old Testament Library* series; Philadelphia: Westminster Press, 1974), 183.

7. Brevard Childs, *Isaiah* (*The Old Testament Library* series; Louisville, KY: Westminster John Knox Press, 2001), 179.

8. See http://climate.nasa.gov/key_indicators (accessed May 12, 2014).

9. See http://www.suncomeup.com (accessed May 12, 2014).

10. C. D. Woodroffe, "Reef-island topography and the vulnerability of atolls to sea-level rise," *Global and Planetary Change* Vol. 62 (May 2008): 77-96. See also *National Geographic* video, "Global Warming: Tuamotus."

11. See the 2014 report from the Intergovernmental Panel on Climate Change (IPCC).

12. For more information, see http://epa.gov/climatestudents/impacts/signs/sea-level.html (accessed May 12, 2014).

13. This is essentially the way that Paul understood divine judgment in Romans 1:18 ff., writing that "the wrath of God is revealed from heaven against all ungodliness and wickedness of those who by their wickedness suppress the truth" (v. 18). In essence, the divine judgment consists in God giving people over or giving them up to pursue their lusts—which in fact prove to be their undoing, their dissolution and destruction. Sin pays its just wage in death (vv. 18-32); simply put, sin kills.

14. R. K. Pachauri, "Climate Change 2007: Synthesis Report" (2008).

Chapter 4

1. Irenaeus, *Against Heresies*, Book IV, Chaps. XXXVII-XXXIX, in *Ante-Nicene Fathers*, Vol. 1, eds. Alexander Roberts and James Donaldson (Peabody, MA: Hendrickson Publishers, 1995), 518-23.

2. Ibid., Book V, Chap. VI.1, 531-32.

3. Good examples of parallelism would include, among a great many others, "Do not cast me away from your presence, and do not take your holy spirit from me" (Ps. 51:11) and "Before she was in labor she gave birth; before her pain came upon her she delivered a son" (Isa. 66:7).

4. Irenaeus, *Against Heresies*, Book III, Chap. XI.3, 427.

5. Ibid., Book V, Chap. I.2, 527.

6. Ibid.

7. Ibid., Book V, Chap. II.2 and 3, 528.

8. Ignatius of Antioch, "To the Smyrnaeans," c. 6, in *The Apostolic Fathers* (New York: Christian Heritage, 1947), 121, 120.

9. From fragments attributed to Apollinaris in "Exposition of the Divine Incarnation in the Likeness of Man," ed. H. Lietzmann, *Apollinaris von Laodicea und seine Schule, TU,* i. (Tübingen: J. C. B. Mohr, 1904).

10. Gregory of Nazianzus, "To Cledonius against Apollinaris" (Epistle 101), *The Library of Christian Classics,* Volume III: *Christology of the Later Fathers,* ed. Edward Rochie Hardy (Philadelphia: Westminster Press, 1954), 218-19.

11. Ibid., 219.

12. See chapter 3 of this book, pages 57-60.

13. We are increasingly convinced that this understanding of "flesh" sheds significant light on Paul's usage of the term *sarx.* "Flesh" is not in itself evil or sinful; it is only when people "live in accordance with the flesh" (e.g., Rom. 8:5)—that is, live as though only the visible, creaturely realm is real and true—that they are in a fallen state. So, simply, the realm of the flesh is not the problem, for it is nothing other than the realm of finite, frail creaturehood. If it were the problem, an evil condition in and of itself, then it would be ludicrous to believe that "the Word became flesh." The problem, again, is "living *according to* the flesh," or limiting our vision, our hopes, our loves, our agenda to this creaturely realm and what we can accomplish or gain within it by our feverish grasping.

14. Robert Louis Wilken, *The Spirit of Early Christian Thought: Seeking the Face of God* (New Haven, CT: Yale University Press, 2003), 113.

15. We might note, too, that the heretical Christology of Apollinaris falls flat in the light of this story, especially as Matthew tells it: "My Father, if it is possible, let this cup pass from me" (Matt. 26:39), Jesus prayed. If we take the language of the text seriously, we realize that Jesus did not know for certain—at least in this moment very near the end of his earthly ministry!—whether or not it was possible.

16. Cited by Wilken, *Spirit of Early Christian Thought,* 129.

17. Maximus cited in ibid., 131.

18. Wilken, *Spirit of Early Christian Thought,* 131.

19. Maximus the Confessor, *Difficulty 41,* as cited in Ian A. McFarland, ed., *Creation and Humanity: The Sources of Christian Theology* (Louisville, KY: Westminster John Knox Press, 2009), 124.

20. Ibid., 126.

21. Ibid., 127.

Chapter 5

1. These are the opening stanzas of Hymn 104, "Grace before Meat," *Works* 7:211-12. Found originally in the 1739 edition of *Hymns and Sacred Poems,* this hymn of eight stanzas is situated under the section heading "For Mourners Convinced of Sin" in the 1780 *Collection of Hymns.*

2. John Wesley, *A Plain Account of Christian Perfection* (Kansas City: Beacon Hill Press of Kansas City, 1966), 13.

3. John Wesley, "The Image of God," [I].4, in *John Wesley's Sermons: An Anthology,* eds. Albert C. Outler and Richard P. Heitzenrater (Nashville: Abingdon Press, 1991), 14.

4. These are the closing stanzas of Hymn 104, "Grace before Meat," *Works* 7:211-12. Those familiar with John Wesley's *A Plain Account of Christian Perfection* may remember that in that work he quotes the final two stanzas as a portrait of the holy life.

5. Further, it is probable that the best interpretation of the phrase "spiritual body" (*soma pneumatika*) would be that the resurrected body is a "body of the Spirit," i.e., a body reanimated and sustained by the life-giving Spirit of God. See N. T. Wright, *Surprised by Hope* (New York: HarperOne, 2008), 43-44.

6. These words come from the second paragraph of the Apostles' Creed, which scholars believe developed during the middle of the second century of the Christian era.

7. It may be instructive to bear in mind that the word "influence" is derived from Latin roots that suggest a "flowing into" another.

8. Wesley, *Plain Account*, 55.

9. See John Wesley's sermons "The Witness of the Spirit" (published 1746) and "The Witness of the Spirit (II)" (1767). They are found, respectively, in his *Works* (Nashville: Abingdon, 1984) 1:269-84 and 285-98.

10. From Article IV in the Church of England's Thirty-Nine Articles of Religion, first published in 1562. This phrase reflects the universal church's conviction regarding the resurrection state of the Incarnate Word. Hence, the wording is identical in Article III ("Of the Resurrection of Christ") of the United Methodist Church's Articles of Religion and in Article II ("Jesus Christ") in the Church of the Nazarene *Manual*'s Articles of Faith.

11. Wesley, *Plain Account*, 11, 38, 117. This was one of Wesley's favored characterizations of the sanctified Christian life—essentially quotations from Philippians 2:5 and 1 John 2:6 that, in Wesley's interpretation, speak to the necessity of "inward" and "outward" holiness.

12. John Wesley, "The Scripture Way of Salvation," I.1, in *John Wesley's Sermons*, 372.

13. "The Great Assize," IV.5, ibid., 323.

14. "The One Thing Needful," I.2, ibid., 35.

15. Ibid., II.5, 37.

16. "Original Sin," III.5, ibid., 334.

17. "The Means of Grace," [I].2, ibid., 158.

18. It is significant, too, that the church's traditional method of ordination is by "the laying on of hands." Thus, the human body and human touch are perceived to be a significant avenue for the communication of the Spirit's presence, power, and authority. Similarly, the same gospel that proclaims that "the Word became flesh and lived among us" (John, in 1:14) is also the only one that narrates Jesus's washing of his disciples' feet after his Last Supper with them (John 13:1-11). It is arguable that Jesus's command that his followers "also ought to wash one another's feet" (v. 14) is indicative of the importance of human touch for a community that proclaims the reality of the incarnation of the Word (vv. 12-17)—a community that testifies not only of "what we have heard" or even "what we have seen with

our eyes," but of "what we . . . have touched with our hands, concerning the word of life" (1 John 1:1).

19. *John Wesley's Sermons*, III.12, 165.

20. Ibid., I.1, 15. For a helpful discussion of Wesley's understanding of human "affections," see Randy L. Maddox, *Responsible Grace: John Wesley's Practical Theology* (Nashville: Abingdon Press, 1994), 68-70.

21. For a classic formulation of this argument, see Karl Barth, *Christ and Adam: The Human and Humanity in Romans 5* (New York: Collier Books, 1962).

22. "The Image of God," I.2, *John Wesley's Sermons*, 15-16.

23. See Wesley's sermon "The General Deliverance," [I].1, *Works* 6:241.

24. J. Wesley, "Upon Our Lord's Sermon on the Mount, Discourse I," I.11, ibid., 5:256.

25. "The Circumcision of the Heart," [I].3, *John Wesley's Sermons*, 24.

26. See this phrase's repeated usage, for example, in Wesley, *Plain Account*, 90-92.

27. "The One Thing Needful," II.2, *John Wesley's Sermons*, 36.

28. Ibid., 37.

29. Ibid., 38. Wesley draws the perhaps surprising language of "partakers of the divine nature" from 2 Peter 1:4 (KJV).

30. A beautiful hymn of brother Charles that celebrates the conviction that "God is Love" (among many others) is his "Wrestling Jacob," with the repeated chorus of praise, "Thy Nature, and Thy Name, is Love." For full text, see *Thy Nature and Thy Name Is Love: Wesleyan and Process Theologies in Dialogue*, eds. Bryan P. Stone and Thomas Jay Oord (Nashville: Abingdon Press, 2001), 21.

31. "The New Birth," I.1, *John Wesley's Sermons*, 336.

32. Ibid.

33. See chapter 4 of this book, 70-72.

34. See Wesley, "The General Deliverance," I.5, *Works* 6:244-45.

35. "The New Birth," I.1, *John Wesley's Sermons*, 336.

36. Wesley, "The General Deliverance," I.3, *Works* 6:244.

37. Theodore Runyon, *The New Creation: John Wesley's Theology Today* (Nashville: Abingdon Press, 1988), 17.

38. "The New Birth," I.1, *John Wesley's Sermons*, 337.

39. Ibid., 336.

Chapter 6

1. Martin Buber, *I and Thou*, trans. Walter Kaufmann (New York: Touchstone, 1971), 131.

2. See chapter 3 of this book.

3. We might even wonder about the fact that, increasingly in the past few decades, Christian eschatology has recovered the biblical proclamation that *all of creation* will be renewed and redeemed. But as our understanding of the immensity of creation continues to be expanded, our minds blown, by the incalculable size of the universe with its billions of galaxies, we ought to wonder: Does the new creation that Jesus announced and embodied apply, somehow, to distant galaxies?

We read in Colossians that through Christ "God was pleased to reconcile to himself all things, whether on earth or in heaven, by making peace through the blood of his cross" (1:20)—but how far-reaching is "heaven" in this instance?

4. Charles Wesley, "Hymns for Whit-Sunday," No. 28, in Charles and John Wesley, *Hymns of Petition and Thanksgiving for the Promise of the Father* (1746).

5. Wesley, "The General Spread of the Gospel," *Works* 6:277.

6. Ibid., 279.

7. B. Ozkaynak, et al., "Scenarios and Sustainability Transformation," in *Global Environment Outlook 5: Environment for the Future We Want*, eds. Matthew Billot, et al. (Malta: United Nations Environment Programme, 2013), http://www.unep.org/geo/geo5.asp (accessed May 12, 2014).

8. Ibid.

9. "Living Planet Report 2012: Biodiversity, Biocapacity and Better Choices," *WWF, Switzerland*, http://awsassets.panda.org/downloads/1_lpr_2012_online_full_size_single_pages_final_120516.pdf (accessed May 12, 2014).

10. Wesley, "General Spread," 279.

11. Ibid.

12. Ibid.

13. Ibid., 279-80.

14. Ibid., 280.

15. Ibid.

16. Catherine Keller, "Salvation Flows: Eschatology for a Feminist Wesleyanism," *Quarterly Review* Vol. 23, No. 4 (Winter 2003), 416. Her citation of the phrase "react upon" comes from Wesley's sermon "The Great Privilege of Those Who Are Born of God," where he speaks of grace as "a continual action of God upon the soul" and the human response of gratitude, obedience, and prayer as "the re-action of the soul upon God."

17. See, for example, Wesley's sermon "Free Grace," *Works* 7:373-86. This understanding of divine grace is at the heart of Maddox's *Responsible Grace*.

18. Irenaeus, *Against Heresies*, Book V, Chap. I.2, 527.

19. See chapter 3 of this book.

20. Wesley, "General Spread," 280.

21. Ibid.

22. The eminent American theologian Paul van Buren once mused that it "seems unlikely, having made the commitment and self-limiting move entailed in having begun this creation, that [God's] final goal were to be rid of it; but who knows? Perhaps for God, too, enough can be enough," in *A Theology of the Jewish-Christian Reality, Part I: Discerning the Way* (San Francisco: Harper & Row, 1980), 200.

23. See chapter 3, pp. 57-60.

24. Wesley, "General Spread," 280.

25. Ibid.

26. Wesley, comment on 1 John 4:8 in his *Explanatory Notes upon the New Testament* (London: Epworth Press, 1976), 914.

27. Wesley, "General Spread," 281.

28. Ibid., 280. Italics are Wesley's.

29. Ibid. Italics are Wesley's.

30. B. Ozkaynak, L. Pinter, D. P. van Vuuren, et al., http://www.unep.org/geo/geo5.asp (accessed May 12, 2014).

31. Ibid.

32. Wesley, "The General Deliverance," III.2, *Works* 6:248.

33. Ibid., 244.

34. Ibid., 243.

35. Ibid., 251.

36. Ibid.

37. Ibid., 251-52.

38. We do know that the rabbinic tradition was already developing the language of "the birth-pangs of the Messiah," that is, that as the coming of the Messiah was increasingly near, the world's sufferings and sorrows were also increasing. See M. Lodahl, *God of Nature and of Grace: Reading the World in a Wesleyan Way* (Nashville: Abingdon Press, 2003), 207-12.

39. Keller, "Salvation Flows," 416.

40. Wesley, "General Spread," 288.

41. Ibid., 287.

Chapter 7

1. See Lauren Winner's wonderful meditations in *Mudhouse Sabbath: An Invitation to a Life of Spiritual Discipline* (Brewster, MA: Paraclete Press, 2003); Barbara Brown Taylor offers compelling insights into Sabbath observance in "The Practice of Saying No," chap. 8 of her *An Altar in the World: A Geography of Faith* (New York: HarperCollins, 2009).

2. Gail R. O'Day, *The Gospel of John: Introduction, Commentary, and Reflections* in *The New Interpreter's Bible*, Vol. IX (Nashville: Abingdon Press, 1995), 608.

3. Irenaeus, *Against Heresies*, in *The Library of Christian Classics*, Volume I: *Early Christian Fathers*, trans. and ed. Cyril C. Richardson (Philadelphia: Westminster Press, 1953), 380-81.

The Eighth Day

1. Arthur Stanley, "Lord! It Is Good for Us to Be," in John Wesley, *A Collection of Hymns for the Use of the People Called Methodists, with a New Supplement* (London: Wesleyan Conference Office, 1877), hymn no. 698.

Find Yourself in the Incredible Story of God

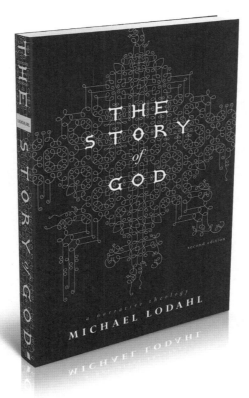

THE BIBLE is filled with amazing stories, but even more amazing is its overarching account of God. It's a story that, despite its twists and turns, portrays God's mercy and love and never-ending effort to connect with God's people.

Drawing from Scripture, everyday experience, and contemporary reflection, Michael Lodahl weaves together the stories and themes of the Bible to present a compelling picture of the grand story of God and God's amazing love.

The Story of God
Michael Lodahl
978-0-8341-2393-9

Also available in ebook format

BEACON HILL PRESS
OF KANSAS CITY

Available online at BeaconHillBooks.com

RETHINK YOUR PART
IN THE WORLD

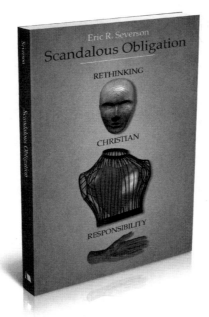

Scandalous Obligation is driven by the sense that there is something profoundly wrong with the way responsibility is developed in the world today. Eric Severson delves into the slippery nature of obligation, the competing calls to justice, and the perilous temptation to dismiss and avoid responsibility.

Scandalous Obligation is a must-read challenge for communities and individuals to take responsibility for the broken bodies, empty plates, and leaking roofs of the world and to be bound to the faces that surround us.

"*Scandalous Obligation* is a wake-up call to a church grown self-absorbed and complacent."
—Karl Giberson
Vice President, BioLogos Foundation
Coauthor, *The Language of Faith and Science*

Scandalous Obligation
978-0-8341-2612-1

Also available in ebook format

BEACON HILL PRESS
OF KANSAS CITY

Available online at BeaconHillBooks.com